Philadelphia. Hance brothers & White

How to make your window pay your rent

being a series of money making designs for window display and store

decoration

Philadelphia. Hance brothers & White

How to make your window pay your rent
 being a series of money making designs for window display and store decoration

ISBN/EAN: 9783744737319

Printed in Europe, USA, Canada, Australia, Japan

Cover: Foto ©Lupo / pixelio.de

More available books at **www.hansebooks.com**

HOW TO MAKE YOUR WINDOW PAY YOUR RENT

Being a series of money making designs for window display and store decoration, to which are appended some general ideas of practical utility.

Hance Brothers & White
Pharmaceutical Chemists
Philadelphia

50999
HANCE BROTHERS & WHITE

Cable address " HANCEBROS "
" A B C " code fourth edition

HEAD OFFICE

CALLOWHILL AND MARSHALL STREETS
PHILADELPHIA
LONG DISTANCE 'PHONE NO. 1840

LABORATORY

Callowhill Marshall Seventh and Willow Streets
Philadelphia

BRANCH OFFICES

New York   Seabury Building 59-61 Maiden Lane
LONG DISTANCE 'PHONE NO. 4195 " CORTLANDT "

Chicago   195 E Randolph Street
LONG DISTANCE 'PHONE NO. 3007 " MAIN "

Pittsburg   419 Seventh Avenue
LONG DISTANCE 'PHONE NO. 33

London   124 Southwark Street, S. E.

How to Take the Laziness Out of Your Window

It's a lazy thing, that window of yours ; a very lazy thing. It won't even keep itself clean, to say nothing of actively aiding you in money making. Many a druggist who is quite alive to the necessity of a clean window, stops right there and utterly fails to make his window work.

There should not be a lazy inch in your entire store, least of all, in that space which could work twenty-four hours of the day, without getting tired, if you only m. ⅔ it attend to business.

In the pages that follow, we offer suggestions enough of what other people have done with their windows, to help you to make *your* window bestir itself to the point of profit. We shall easily be able to show you that these exhibits were in many cases the very making of the stores that used them ; that druggists who enthusiastically adopted our entire program were dubbed "The Frog Man" of their neighborhood, and that the title of this book, "How to Make Your Window Pay Your Rent," is no exaggeration.

EVOLUTION OF THE SHOW WINDOW

Not many things spring into being in the full development of all their powers and usefulness. The chimney began with a hole in the roof ; it was improved until finally we had a chimney that would draw.

The obvious need for "light on the subject" was the necessity that mothered the invention of the window ; and from a window that was only useful for letting in light have been evolved windows, that, like chimneys, will draw, that is to say, will attract trade and pay the rent. When the first house was built, its tenants saw at once that they couldn't dwell in darkness. So they made rude holes in the walls to admit light.

From that primitive makeshift down to the present splendors of plate-glass and bronze and marble is a "far cry"—too far a cry to record here. We could tell you, if we had the time, of the gradual growth of the window ; of the use of thin sheets of horn and oiled paper as window lights, of the tiny thick-framed panes that marked the windows of the past.

The drugstore window has grown, like the rest. From a hole in the wall it has developed into a commercial necessity—an actual salesman, counted by the wise druggist as one of his foremost sources of profit.

Our retail drug ancestors—lots of professional etiquette and little money in those days—used their small-paned windows to admit light to their stores ; they gave them no other thought. Strange as it seems, there are druggists alive now who do the same thing ; they belong so far in the past that they look on their windows as mere holes in the wall to let in light or, confidentially, even worse—as a sort of accommodating waste-basket to hold things for which no better room can be found under counter or shelf.

Many years ago, an old-time "chemist," as he would probably have called himself (he would have been the most "individual" druggist of his town had he lived in our day), made the discovery that by putting in his windows bottles containing blue, pink, green and orange-colored compounds,—his townspeople could see, without half trying, that his was a drugstore. It was a curious thought, but it took root. The practice grew rapidly. Colored glass globes soon became the druggist's symbol. The vivid spheres attracted attention. Men, women and children stopped in the street to look at these first crude window displays.

Here was step No. 1 in the evolution of the window: it had begun to be of some commercial value to its owner.

This early druggist soon conceived the idea of placing the simple night-light he used behind the globes, so that far up and down the street until the early bed hours of those days the gleaming colored lights pointed the way to "ye apothecarie's shoppe."

From colored bottles to the placing of goods in the window was but a step "If people are attracted by meaningless glass globes, why not by goods?" And so one day a druggist-philosopher conceived the idea of putting in his window some neat, fresh packages of goods, instead of placing them all on his shelves. This was a breach of etiquette and conservatism that made his competitors first gasp with astonishment, then glower with anger, for the goods sold faster than they had ever done before.

Here was step No. 2: the window had begun to pay the rent.

Soon the flat narrow window became inadequate. Succeeding generations saw that the small panes and their heavy frames obscured the effect. Then was born the genuine bulk window with its mighty panes of French plate.

This was the real beginning of the science of window dressing. The druggist, who now counts his window among his salesmen, can thank his professional ancestor whose wild dream of sensational enterprise was the filling of glass bottles with red, green and blue water.

The successors of the man who first put goods in his window have been many and varied in kind; indeed the show windows of the country at this present day show every phase of development from the most crude and useless except as light-admitters, up to those of the merchant princes, who sacrifice light, doorways and space, and spend enormous sums of money in order to reap the full advantage of the value which they know their windows possess.

[We break off in this narrative to open a letter from the top of a pile. The letter is one of inquiry. The druggist who wrote it wishes to know something about our goods. He wants particularly to know whether they lend themselves well to window displays. He has cultivated his window to such an extent, he says, that it will sell anything salable that can be displayed in it. He concludes by asking whether our goods are the sort he can use for window display. That druggist doesn't know that we were pioneers in instructing druggists in window display, though he will before we are through with him. He doesn't know either that the most of our specialties are packed with the special view of being displayed in a window, but he will know that, too, in a little while.]

Examples of the value placed on window-advertising by successful merchants, might be multiplied almost indefinitely ; two conspicuous ones are probably sufficient, however, and they are familiar to all Philadelphians.

THE "HOSPITABLE OPEN DOOR" IDEA

A clothing store was built of mammoth dimensions and with a correspondingly wide entrance, on the supposition of making it easy to walk in at. The man who saw "Oak Hall" five years ago, and hasn't seen it since, wouldn't recognize it to-day. Then its first floor was "all door." The "hospitable open door" was all they considered *necessary* to draw business. The time came, however, when that ceased to be enough. The proprietors discovered that the easiest way to get buyers into the store was to make the windows attractive with displays of goods. Buyers were compelled to come in. The size of the door was then found to make little difference, and so the greater part of the door space was turned into more window space.

All the doors but one were taken out. In their place came a long line of magnetic windows. Heavy steel girders were introduced to support the upper floors, and were skilfully and artistically concealed by mirrors, which of course intensified the advertising effect by seeming to multiply the images which they reflected. To-day practically the whole of the first two stories of "Oak Hall" are of clear plate-glass—the first floor windows showing a score of oft-changed window displays ; the second floor windows the busy-selling scenes within.

The "hospitable open door" was all right once ; its day is done. "Oak Hall" had doors enough to admit 50,000 people—and no windows to draw them. They had a splendid basket for the fish they wanted to catch but no bait. Things are different now. A modern merchant knows, without telling, that a good show window will get the people into his store, no matter if the door is around the corner and only three feet wide.

A DOUBLE-DECKER

The huge building now occupied by Gimbel Brothers, at Ninth and Market Streets, is another good example of window development. Their predecessors had the corner rounded directly at the apex, with a huge door in the centre. At that time this was considered a shrewd bid for the passing trade both ways—down Market and up and down Ninth. And it served its purpose very well. But when Gimbel Brothers, merchants of a later generation, took the store, they saw no merit in the hospitable mammoth double door on the ground floor. They at once built out to their full line. The first-floor corner they turned into a huge glittering show window that holds as much goods as many a country store. The lofty door at the corner gave place to smaller doors on either side, and the space thus saved went to the enormous corner show windows. The corner of Gimbel Brothers' building is now really an immense two-story show window, gleaming and glittering by day and night—a splendid monument to the new order of commercial things. It wouldn't be true to say that Gimbel Brothers, purely by the increase in their show window space, were enabled in less than ten years to build up a business increase far larger than their predecessor's whole business after fifty years of laborious effort ; but that undoubtedly helped in the work, and Gimbel Brothers knew it would when they went to the expense of a change.

EXAMPLES FROM NEWSPAPERDOM

Here are conspicuous examples of the same tendency from an entirely different field. The newspapers are enterprising enough about some things— extremely obtuse about others. They have been among the last to recognize that they, too, could use a show window ; but their eyes are open at last. The metropolitan dailies are coming forth from their cellars. They are letting the public into the secret of their inner workings. They are building show windows for themselves. The *New York Herald* is a conspicuous example. Travelers in New York are familiar with the *Herald's* magnificent press room, with floor in cellar, but ceiling twenty feet above the ground level. The walls are of plate-glass, and one can see clear across the massive presses from one street to the other, a square away.

The *Herald* has made of its first two floors a mighty show window. In it it has placed the splendid electrical machinery which prints the thousands of its circulation. Tardily the paper has come to realize the advertising value which lies in interesting people in what you have—in you and your business.

The *Evening Bulletin*, of Philadelphia, is following the same plan. Its basement at Sixth and Chestnut Streets, was formerly consecrated to the sale of trunks and traveling bags. Now huge presses whir and spin there. The interested people view their wondrous evolutions through immense plate-glass windows, installed not so much to admit light as to allow sight of the public. We venture the prophecy that the time will come when the big newspapers will take the public still further into their confidence—when they will set up type-setting machines in their windows and in the full gaze of the attracted public will cast the little metal letters that spell the daily history of the world.

Verily the old order of things is passing away. Go anywhere in any city you like, you will see old store fronts being replaced by new. You will note that an invariable characteristic of the new is large bulk windows that almost seem at times over-large for the front. Some of these modern store fronts show wonderful windows that would probably be ashamed to confess kinship with the original ancient hole in the wall. Windows of crystal and without wood, their parts held together by nickel bolts; windows of fanciful shapes and patterns; windows of such clear glass that they seem uncovered—yet all partaking of the common object—the showing and the sale of goods. The old merchant's window admitted light only, and not a great deal of that. The new merchant's window admits light and business, too.

A $100 BOOK

For this book we ask a painstaking and careful perusal. It has cost us thousands of dollars in the acquirement of its contents and its preparation, and if we were not sure that it could be made of more than $100 value to you, we would not have issued it.

May we say that such a book as this, which represents the best thought of many intelligent minds, and years of discriminating selection among many excellent suggestions, cannot be digested at a single reading? And may we further suggest that whenever you are planning a striking display, you first take this book and look over its pages as a preliminary to your work? You will find the time well spent.

AN INVITATION

We would have liked very much, had there been time, to show illustrations of window-transfigurations like those described above. Such illustrations, however, could not have done their subjects justice, so they would not have been of much use after all.

The best thing for a druggist to do who is interested in the development of show windows is to visit New York or Philadelphia and see for himself.

And Philadelphia will teach him far more in this respect than New York could do. This city affords scores of examples quite as noteworthy as those which have been mentioned. There has been greater appreciation in Philadelphia of the value of window space and keener competition among merchants to give their windows every possible advantage—for advertising and selling their wares. Come, therefore, and see for yourself; it will pay you.

Hance Brothers & White.

"Frog in your Throat?" 10¢

THE GREATEST COUGH LOZENGE ON EARTH

A FINE WINDOW DISPLAY OF TEN-CENTS-ABLES

SUGGESTION FOR A NOVEL DISPLAY

CHAPTER I

What Windows Are

The subject of window dressing as a means of increasing a druggist's income has ceased to be a question of theory with us.

We have seen the idea so often used, with splendid results, that it is a source of continual wonder to us how any druggist can ignore the opportunities that lie before him. If perseverance can do it, however, the time will come when the druggist indifferent upon this subject will be looked upon as a curiosity, genuine and unmistakable.

Your store windows, like eye-glasses, should be made to properly fit you. Through one you see the world; through the other the world sees you.

The first step to a successful grasp of the subject is to realize what a window is. Look for one moment at the windows of any private house in a residential street in the city. What are they? They are sign-boards which tell you what sort of people live inside. One person in one hundred may cross the threshold and see the inmates of that house, but the remaining ninety-nine must look at the windows, and imagine from their appearance what style of persons are living behind them.

Your windows may do you great harm. You may be a person of fine instincts, of exquisite discernment, of wonderful patience, of sound judgment; but your neighbors know nothing of this. They can only judge by what they see. And what do they see as they walk by your house every day? They look at your windows and judge you accordingly.

Thus windows are tell-tales. They proclaim you to the world. They are a perpetual announcement of the taste of the unseen dwellers behind them. Perhaps eight hundred persons will pass your house to-day. Fifty of them know you personally. But seven hundred and fifty look at your windows and take their cue from them. Now leave the house and come to your store windows. Your store window really introduces you to your customers. Is it the sort of introduction you would have? Does it vouch for the dignity and character of your establishment? You are careful how you address a new customer; but your store window addresses him as forcibly as your words.

And it addresses him oftener. It addresses him earlier, before your personality has had a chance to help you. Your window has the first chance at him. And first impressions are lasting!

DISPLAY OF MR. JOHN B. EDIE, McKEESPORT, PA.

Who is responsible for the appearance of your store windows? Are you getting from them all the help you can? Are they doing you any good? Are you certain that they are not quietly doing you harm?

These are potent questions. You can afford to give time to their consideration. They have had our most careful thought for years. Let them have your whole attention for an hour.

Do not mind if we tread a little upon your toes at times. You are grasping a big thought, and every live thought on any live subject knocks the wind out of somebody or other. We want to make you dissatisfied with the slow growth of your business as it now stands. Do you remember the greatest compliment (so it is claimed) ever paid by a king to one of his subjects? It was what Louis XIV, the *grand monarque* of France, said to his priest Masillon, "Father, I have heard many great preachers, and I have been satisfied with them; but as for you, whenever I hear you it makes me dissatisfied with myself." So if our stout expressions can only make you dissatisfied with your neglect of window displays, forgive the advocate his plea, and remember that his only object is to make your ledger more interesting reading in the near future.

CHAPTER II

What a Druggist has to do with Window Display

The first plunge into the subject is almost a cold shiver. It looks at first sight as if there might be something undignified in a druggist bothering with dressing windows. Do you recall the story of the hen who looked at the china egg in her nest in a distrustful way, and ejaculated: "Great Scott, if this sort of thing goes on I'll be a bricklayer next." How many druggists look distrustfully at the idea of a good window display, and feel that if that undignified sort of thing goes on they might as well become sandwich-men without further delay.

Don't be unreasonable. You have a beautiful and perfectly unnecessary notion that you will sink your dignity in your efforts at window display. Let us stare that idea right out of countenance here. *Never need dignity be sacrificed.* On the contrary, unless your window display be made with a scrupulous regard for dignity (as expressed by good taste), you will derive little benefit from it. Dignity always. Dignity or nothing.

But not over-dignity. That is simply ridiculous. You remember the over-dignified dentist. He hated the very

DISPLAY OF MESSRS. NICHOLS & HARRIS, NEW LONDON, CONN.

name of "dentist," and so he left it off his business card altogether and inserted instead, "Drawing, Music, and Dancing :—No pains spared."

Granting the dignity of it, then why should a druggist take any time for a window display? *Simply because he is in business to make money.* No descendant of Shem, Ham or Japheth can do any less and stay in business. If men kept drugstores for their health, or for enjoyment, or for social prestige, it would be well enough to ignore window display, although the most important contributor to the dignity of the drugstore would thereby be ignored.

But men are in business to make money, and they must do considerable help-yourself fighting. When the little girl was asked who made her, she held up her apron, saying, "God made me that length, and I grew the rest myself." Now, the fact that you keep a drugstore on a prominent street will bring you in a certain amount of custom, perhaps a living. But your location and business make you that length without your help. If you want anything more than a living, you must grow the rest yourself. In all business, as a rule, men can afford to employ any honest method to make money. A druggist can afford to employ any dignified method.

Window display is such a method. This is not a question of opinion; it is a question of *fact* The records stand open for all to read. Figures cannot lie. Thousands of druggists have tried window display. A hundred of them show you the way to try it in the pages of this book.

The subject is timely. "Favors lose their value by delay." The movement of ideas over this country comes in great waves. If you start in ahead of the bulk or volume of the great movement you are thrown forward strongly by it, exactly as you would be thrown ahead by a wave if you got in front of the bulk of water. So of a clear idea like window display in the drug business. Where there was one druggist who did it in '93, there were twenty who started it in '94. Nearly four hundred more joined the procession in '95; there will be four thousand who will be doing it next year. Don't delay. Make the partnership that Charles V made when he cried, "Myself and the lucky moment." Remember the old law maxim that rights are forfeited by disuse. Claim your right immediately. Make a splendid window display of " Frog in your Throat?"

Speaking about delays, reminds us of the story of the

minister who was called to another parish, but who had not been able to make up his mind whether to go or not. The deacon of the parish met the minister's little boy playing in the road, and asked him if his father had decided. "Yes," said the boy, "father's going to leave you." "Indeed," said the deacon, "I didn't know that he had made up his mind yet." "Well," said the boy, "you see it's like this. Father, he's in his room all the time a praying for light; but mother—*she's packing the trunks!*"

You don't want to sit any longer praying for business while we are packing the trunks daily with "Frog in your

you remember how Sir Walter Raleigh once made a wager with Queen Elizabeth that he could weigh the smoke from his pipe? He won by weighing the tobacco before smoking and the ashes afterward. You can weigh the value of your window display by weighing your money drawer before and after.

A good window display will stimulate your general business as a tonic stimulates appetite. It will bring new customers into your store. You can better afford it than half the expenses you incur. It will easily show a forty to fifty per cent increase in your total sales. *Provided you do it rightly.*

DISPLAY OF MR. JOHN COLEMAN, WHEELING, W. VA.

Throat?" outfits to go to other druggists who have decided to make displays. Therefore, take this matter up here and now; come to some definite conclusion. Don't merely set it aside to settle itself. Such things never can settle themselves. When a physician and a surgeon once disagreed as to the wisdom of performing an operation, the surgeon said, "Very well, let it settle itself, but the postmortem will show I am right."

You don't want to wait for post-mortem decisions. Decide it now. Don't ignore it. Don't default on the answer. Don't leave your good resolution uncorked to grow inactive.

We say again: *It is results that tell the story!* Do

For in window display, as in every other art, there are things to be avoided and things to be carefully provided. There are many ways of missing the goal; there is only one travelled way to attain it. Let us run over the experiments of others and note a few important axioms as they come to us from the hand of Experience.

CHAPTER III

Using One Article as the Basis of the Display

This is virtually saying to the public that although you have five hundred articles to show them, this one thing is so important that for it you put all other things aside. You thus place such a heavy emphasis on one

DISPLAY OF FIFTH AVE. DRUG CO., BROOKLYN, N. Y.

article that you arouse interest in it, you excite curiosity immediately as to its merits, and provoke sales which could never be made under normal conditions with ordinary surroundings.

Men say, " what is this thing? why should it occupy such attention?" Their questions remain unanswered, and they probe the subject further. They make inquiries, and four out of five such inquiries end in sales.

You create a "run" on the one article displayed, and a "run" is simply a rolling snowball of trade. The further it rolls the more snow it attracts, and about the easiest way to get rich yet discovered is to start a "run" on any article you are handling.

Some people will tell you that this idea of one subject only in the window display is wrong. Do not let that trouble you. The value of a clever idea for making money is in proportion to the fewer number of people who grasp it. Go back to that line in your St. Augustine, " *Sanitatis patrocinium est, insanientium turba :* "— the multitude of fools is a protection to the wise.

Greece, so much praised for her wisdom, produced but seven wise men ; judge of the number of fools, and remember that the proportion is not much altered to-day.

You have learned a great deal when you realize that you cannot address the public except with one thing at a time. If you are operating a large department store in the city, this rule has its exception. But in every other case, let no temptation swerve you from this concentration upon one subject. The leading experts in advertising all give it as their universal testimony that only one article should ever be mentioned in one advertisement. Publishers long ago discarded the old method of enumerating the books of a popular author. It is "one book at a time," and all the emphasis on that.

See this same lesson in all trades. If you make a blade that shall be both a razor and a carving knife, it will fail in its duty as either. It will not shave like a razor nor carve like a knife. You lose at each end in trying to cover both. What is gained in variety is taken out of effectiveness.

Go a step further. Here is a curious phenomenon. Ask any shoe manufacturer and he will tell you that you cannot make men's and women's shoes under the same roof. Women's shoes so produced have an undesirable mannish look, and men's shoes gradually get womanly. This is ridiculous, but it is true. We live in an age of single aims, and success is only another name for the focusing of all your thought and time and study on one thing. The men who can do that are called

DISPLAY OF MESSRS. H. BOWMAN & CO., OAKLAND, CAL.

"specialists," and they command high prices. Be a specialist in your window displays.

Look in any store window in which there are a dozen or more articles, and see how many of those articles are remembered by you five minutes afterward. Rarely do you remember last one, and yet seldom do you fail to remember one. It is always one. It would appear that the mind instinctively sees and grasps one impression, *and stops short just there!* It is a curious psychological or physiological fact, but it is true. If, then, the mind grasps naturally but one object in a window display, the lesson is clear. Display only one article and by the very multiplication and emphasis of that one you produce a magnified sense of its importance in the mind of the beholder. And don't forget that a display of one article, which will be remembered, will be forever afterward associated in the mind of everybody with the store making it. Surely you recognize the business possibilities in this?

Now, just for a moment let us see how these ideas work in actual practice. Mr. Otto Wicke, of Brooklyn, N. Y., tried the one-idea method of window display, and his experience is most worthy of mention. Mr. Wicke

was one of the contestants in our last great window display contest, and won a second prize. The design of his display was of a rustic character. A background was painted showing a cottage, trees and a rough wood fence. All the rest of the window was given up to working out the idea of the "Frogs' Annual Picnic." In the right-hand back corner was a full band. Also a dancing-platform on which several couples of giddy batrachians were shown as twirling in the mazy waltz. In the left-hand corner was a merry-go-round. Here and there seated at tables, on the most natural looking benches, were parties of Frogs feasting. The boulders that lay around were whitewashed and an advertisement of "Frog in your Throat?" written on them in black. In the foreground of the picture a cricket match was taking place, witnessed by a large and distinguished audience, including, no doubt, all the nobility and gentry of Frog Land, gathered together in a gallery on the left.

The idea of his other display was a battle scene, the background being a painted representation of an attack on a castle by an army of Frogs, who appeared about to take it by storm.

Frog in your Throat!" 10¢   "Frog in your Throat?" 10¢   Frog in your

DISPLAY OF MR. JAMES C. MUNDS, WILMINGTON, N. C.

CHAPTER IV

Actual Results of the One-Idea Method

Ever since the time when the possibilities of window advertising first dawned upon us, we have endeavored to impress upon the druggists who used it the necessity, if they would know its value, of keeping an accurate account of results. Mr. Wicke kept a very close account of the sales of " Frog in your Throat?" induced through his window, and is therefore enabled to state exactly what were the results of not complicating his display by using more than one idea. His own letter shall speak for itself as regards the extraordinary success achieved by him through his display. He writes : " Gentlemen : I take pleasure in notifying you of the large amount of ' Frog in your Throat ?' sold on February 10, 1895, in two of my stores, namely, at 1337 Myrtle Avenue, 160 boxes, and at 457 Knickerbocker Avenue, 117 boxes, and I am fully convinced that I reaped such a harvest through my splendid window displays. Further, I will say that I have sold since the 15th day of September, 1894, to the present day, February 15th, 1895, (six months), the enormous amount of 102 gross, and can conscientiously say that ' Frog in your Throat ?' is the leading proprietary medicine of the day."

The foundation for this display was " Frog in your Throat ?" and that was the only object treated in his display That it was successful was evident. 102 gross means over $700 direct profit; but beside this, who can estimate the value of that boom as an advertisement to Mr. Wicke's general business? Think a moment; 14,698 boxes sold means 14,698 customers brought into the store, a very large percentage of whom, no doubt, bought other articles beside their box of " Frog in your Throat ?" 14,698 people, each going out of the store with 10c worth of complete satisfaction. If the same amount of profit were not realized by the sale of other goods to those 14,698 customers brought into the store by " Frog in your Throat ?" it was the druggist's own fault.

Here is another instance, and we have still others. Mr. John Coleman, of Wheeling, Va., also decided to use the one-idea method, and on this basis he made a display sufficiently good to be noticed by three local newspapers, one of the notices being in German

Mr. Coleman himself writes as follows : " It was an elegant get-up, and proved a wonderful attraction, consequently greatly increased my sales. We went into this contest to win a prize; we spared no work, and you will notice the display cost us some money to get up, but we were confident that you would appreciate our efforts." Again he writes : " We have a grand display. Our win-

DISPLAY OF MR. JOS. S. MADISON, TERRE HAUTE, IND.

dow is crowded the whole day with sight-seers, and our customers have complimented us highly for our efforts." It will be seen that right along the full length of this window there has been made a little lake, lined with sheet lead. On the lake is a Frog paddling a Rob Roy canoe. There also floats a large raft bearing a freight of " Frog in your Throat ?" on the top of which sits the Frog Captain under a parasol. The banks of the lake are strewn with stones and moss. On the front side, near the glass, is a large tent, built of boxes. By that you will see an angling Frog. Further on, a party of " sports " sit playing cards, and others amusing themselves in various ways. All of this forms the " Frog in your Throat ?" fishing camp. On the other side of the lake will be seen a veritable prize-ring. There, at the back, sit the spectators, row above row. Down there in the ring are the two combatants, each with his colors around his waist. There also in the corners are the friends of the fighters, with their towels and buckets. We see also the referee with his watch keeping time. Altogether a very ingenious and highly creditable display.

All Frogs, you see ; nothing but Frogs.

If we were to give space here to all the druggists who found dollars in sticking to one idea in their window displays, we would fill all the pages of this large book several times over. We'll give one more instance, and then pass on.

One of the most signal successes won by the one-idea method came to Mr. James A. Hart, of Sing Sing, N. Y. Mr. Hart made two distinct shows, photographs of which he sent us. He received notices of his show from no less than six of the local papers. The idea carried out in the display is that of a great orchestra; the entire bottom part of the window being fitted up with a large choir of Frogs, each holding in his hand, to represent a piece of music, the small primer relating to " Frog in your Throat ?" The witty druggist has entitled this window " The Song of the Frogs at Sing Sing." Another good idea in this display shown in the photo, not reproduced, was a large globe with the " Frog in your Throat ?" sign pasted around it, thus typifying " Frog in your Throat ?" encircling the world.

Mr. Hart himself writes on March 6th : " I am very much pleased with your letter this a. m. announcing the prizes, and that my name appeared among the successful ten winning the third prize. I will take mine in ' Frog in your Throat ?' believing that to be my *nearest*, and I shall ever swear by it. Wishing you and all your preparations every success. You will find my check enclosed for statement."

Mr. Hart spent some pains in investigating the general effect of his display, and writes us later that he " must acknowledge a general business boom during the whole winter, no doubt largely due to ' Frog in your Throat ?' "

He says : " I would be glad to compete again. The idea of devoting an entire window to the display of any *one line of goods* is a good one, and the fact was never pressed home to me so favorably as in the success brought by the display of ' Frog in your Throat ? ' and the sale has kept up remarkably through the summer months, proving ' Frog in your Throat ? ' has come to stay. By carrying out your ideas, I have given a great impetus to my general trade the entire year. Thanks to you and success for ' Frog in your Throat ? ' "

One thing we have urged constantly with reference to window displays for druggists, is that almost invariably a good display will elicit gratuitous newspaper notices, which constitute the *very best newspaper advertising a druggist can possibly have*. Mr. Hart experienced this, for he received two good newspaper notices, which we reproduce below, simply to clinch our argument:

THIRD PRIZE COMES TO SING SING

" Some weeks since one of Druggist James A Hart's show windows was dressed with the insignia of ' Frog in your Throat ? ' in competition for one of the prizes offered by the owners of that proprietary article. There were about seven hundred competitors in the contest, and on due consideration of the photos of each window the judges have awarded third prize to our townsman, who has the hearty congratulations of the *Republican*. The first prize went to Allegheny, Pa., and the second to Brooklyn."—*Sing Sing, N. Y., Republican.*

HART TAKES THIRD PRIZE

" During the past winter Druggist James A. Hart has been using his show windows to advertise specialties in his line of business. He made a great hit in this way pushing the cough medicine known as ' Frog in your Throat ? ', and of the prizes offered by the manufacturers for the handsomest window display, Mr. Hart took the third. There were over seven hundred competitors throughout the country. The first prize was taken by an Allegheny, Pa., druggist, and the second by a dealer in Brooklyn. Hart, like the *Register*, believes in making advertising attractive, and when backed up by the ' know how to do it,' it gets there every time."—*Sing Sing, N. Y., Democrat Register.*

CHAPTER V

Careful Choice of the Article to be Displayed

Some articles are almost impossible to illustrate; others are very easy. We strongly recommend you to begin with our " Frog in your Throat ? " because : (1) it is timely; no remedy is more in demand at this season of the year; (2) it lends itself immediately to illustration; you can get up a whole window of Frogs and they can be arranged in a hundred attitudes and over fifty occupations; and (3) we supply the Frogs in a dozen different styles. The material is all right at hand and it is full of opportunities.

Then, too, Frogs are most ludicrous creatures, and people of all ages will crowd in front of your window at all hours to watch them. There is almost no article you could select that is such a perfect one for a window display. Think of trying to make an enjoyable, lively and exactly appropriate display of Syringes, Castor Oil, or Syrup of Hypophosphites ! Then turn to " Frog in your

Frog your Throat

DRUG STORE

DISPLAY OF MESSRS. FEDERMANN & HALLER, KANSAS CITY, MO

DISPLAY OF MR. CHARLES YOUNG, JOHNSTOWN, PA.

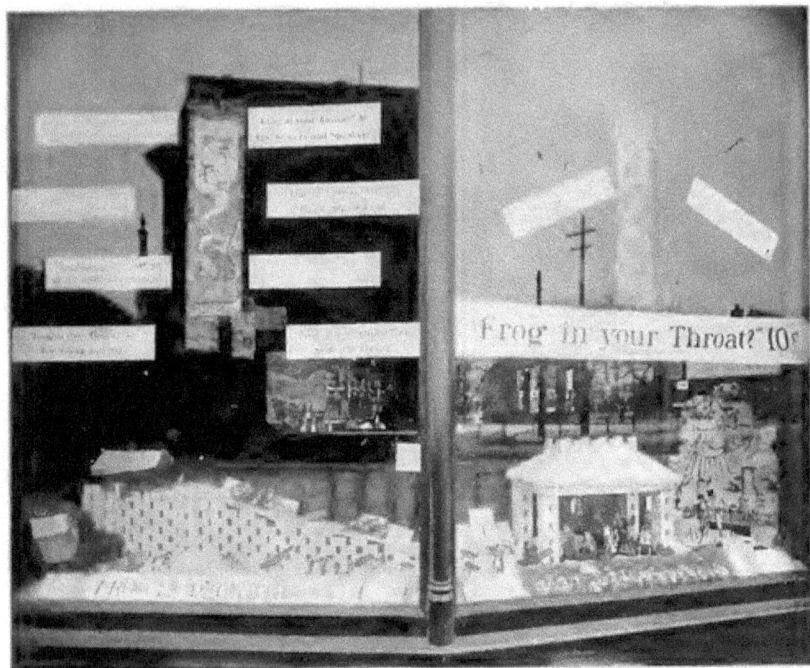

DISPLAY OF MR. F. A. HARTSHORN, MARLBORO, MASS.

Throat?" and, remembering that we furnish an entire Japanese outfit for your use, how many suggestions crowd your mind!

Therefore, take "Frog in your Throat?" for your first effort. Try your hand on it experimentally, and you can be sure of a success in your very initial exhibition. Let it show you whether all that we say about the enormous sales from window displays is true or not. Listen to the comments of customers! Watch the groups all day long in front of your window! Notice how many new customers enter your store! Improve the opportunity for a free notice in your local paper. And if you are still in doubt as to the result, turn to your cash sales and see whether our estimate of a *fifty per cent increase* is too high.

Again, we can show that these ideas are not theories. Many druggists have tried them and have written us of their results. In every case the druggists who have followed out the lines laid down above have made the most conspicuous successes of the total number competing.

Mr. C. A. Uthe, of Norwalk, Ohio, cast about for a subject suitable for an attractive window display, and finally decided upon "Frog in your Throat?" as the best thing he could find. What success he had with it can best be told in Mr. Uthe's own language, descriptive of his display and its results: "In the centre is a basin of water with a running fountain, which throws a jet about 15 inches high. Around the fountain is a wood plank promenade, on which are Frogs walking out, some leaning on the chain which goes around the pond. Another sits fishing on the bank with his basket beside him. On the right of the central pond, a baseball game is in progress, the players being 'Brownies' versus 'Frogs.' Frogs at bat, spectators sitting all around, an umpire, etc., being present. On the left is the dancing-hall with full orchestra, the musicians being all Frogs. Back of it all was fixed with pots of flowers and ferns, and still behind all this a fence was made of tall corn stalks, making a complete summer scene, and a very striking window display. I have had hundreds of compliments, and every one pronounces the display the finest they ever saw." With regard to the effect of the show on the sales, Mr. Uthe writes: "Now, in reference to sales I would say, that 'Frog in your Throat?' is *selling right along all the*

DISPLAY OF MR. E. J. KNOTHE, CHICAGO.

time. I kept no separate account of sales, but I know that the advertising and the display increased my sales over 100 per cent easy enough. Your method of advertising by window display is the best mode of advertising that druggists can adopt, and is far ahead of newspapers, circulars, etc. Through it my general business is on the increase. I never had a display in my window that created so much talk as ' Frog in your Throat?' "

One reason why we have been so successful in showing druggists the advantage of window displays, is because we have something to offer them which adapts itself splendidly to any variety of display they may elect to make. A careful choice of subjects almost invariably brings the chooser down to " Frog in your Throat?"

Mr. James U. Case, of Somerville, N. J., was another of the many who decided to use " Frog in your Throat?" as the article to be displayed in his window. He describes his window as follows: " The window contains a boat house made of boxes of ' Frog in your Throat?,' a Frog pulling a boat from it, and two Frogs carrying the sails. There is a pond of real water with a sail boat on it, being navigated by a Frog mariner. At each corner of the lake

there is a boat, on the top of which there is a light at night. I also have a trapeze performance and a tightrope in the window. There is a large stump in the background, on which several Frogs sit engaged in fishing. Also Frogs around the banks of the pond, in the act of leaping in. To attract people going along the street I have an electric tapper in the window. Several local papers have given me very good puffs, and I am doing very nicely with the sale of ' Frog in your Throat?' "

Mr. Case also received some very valuable newspaper advertising. Two of the notices he received are as follows:

" James U. Case has an attractive window show this week. He has ' seen ' J. C. Field's window and ' gone him one better.' His show is of Frogs, and there is a pond with a sail boat on it, and Frogs are to be seen everywhere. Then on one side is a duck-pond, in which ducks in profusion are to be seen. The scene was made by John D. Case."—*Somerset Democrat.*

" Show-window artists are very active just now in the production of attractive designs for advertising purposes. Thus far the window at Case's pharmacy is considered the most original and unique thing out. It advertised ' Frog in your Throat?' and is represented by a Frog.

pond, with its usual surroundings. To J. D. Case, son of the proprietor, is due the credit of arranging the exhibition."—*Somerset Messenger, Nov. 28, 1894.*

Most druggists are very properly critical about the articles which they display in their windows. That is why so many of them hit upon " Frog in your Throat?" after trying numerous other things. Mr. H. R. Baumann, of Washington, Mo., is one of this latter class. He made a " Frog in your Throat?" display last year, and from his own description of it may be gathered many valuable ideas which can be used with profit by any druggist. He writes : " In the rear to the left of the window rises a mountain on the top of which is built a fort. Moss grows here and there on the mountain and Frogs can be seen perched on the top and sides, whilst a little Frog is making its way to the drawbridge of the fort. Along the foot of the mountain runs a railroad track with a bed of solid gravel. In the right of the window will be seen a railroad train stopping at a station. A Frog is engineer. The train is a mixed one ; one car is a passenger car, with Frog passengers ; the other a freight car, with Frog brakesman. On the platform of the station is a large quantity of boxes of ' Frog in your Throat?' piled up, which has been unloaded, Frog atop of the pile. Driving away from the station is an express wagon, driven by a Frog. This is also loaded with ' Frog in your Throat?' a Frog atop of load. Marching along the track, towards a pond, is a procession of eighteen Frogs, consisting of torch-bearers, musicians, etc. Again, in the right of the window is a ladder with several Frogs atop, and a snake twisted about the lower end. Suspended in mid-air is a double trapeze, with performing Frogs; twined about the upper bar is a snake making its way toward the little Frogs on the small trapeze."

Mr. Baumann found this display one of the best investments he had ever had. Its results justified his choice of a subject. In writing us later he asserts that the display "improved general trade and brought new customers into the store for ' Frog in your Throat?' and these would also purchase other goods which they were in need of. The display," he says, " was the talk of the town, everybody came to see it, and many were the compliments paid us in regard to it. Country people coming to town would stop their wagons and get off to look at the display. For the children it was just a great show ; mothers could not get their little ones away from the window. People would come into the store and inquire what ' Frog in your Throat?' meant, what it was for, and then buy a box."

Do you wonder that we say " choose carefully the article to be displayed," when so much hinges upon it ?

One more instance, and we pass. Mr. Harry C. Stewart, of Wheeling, W. Va., made a display of " Frog in your Throat?" His window was a good one, and he made good use of it. Druggists may reproduce his ideas with profit. He describes his display thus : " My

windows are 6 feet 4 inches wide by 5 feet deep, so you see the display was a large one. I made a garden scene, and labeled it the Frogtown Carnival. On the extreme right was a house built entirely of boxes of ' Frog in your Throat?' set upon a rock surrounded by a stake and rider fence, two steps up to the door. At the window appeared a Frog with a night cap on. Arranged on the moss under the window was the ' Celebrated Frogtown Band' serenading the lady at the window. The band was composed of seven members; three playing accordions, three horns, and one the violin. A path of white sand 6 inches wide leads from the door of the house clear around the garden. In the centre was the fountain and pond; the pond being 2 feet square and 2 inches deep, lined with moss and rocks, containing Frogs, and in the middle of the pond was the fountain. Arranged on a base 1 foot high, made of rocks and moss, was a statue a foot in height, and it held a stand pipe, from which water flowed all the time. The stream was kept going about 2 feet above the statue, so it made a fine appearance. On the bank, in the centre of the window, were four Frogs engaged in the great American game of ' Draw Poker,' using ' Frog in your Throat?' lozenges for chips. To the left, on the stump, were Mr. and Mrs. Josiah Allen and family with the baby in Mrs. Allen's arms. Grouped around over the mound along the path everywhere were Frogs in different attitudes. One pair were out for a walk. He was dressed in a red necktie and a smile, and she had a half-mast skirt on. Altogether, it was the largest display we ever had in this end of the city. Twice I was compelled to ask for police to keep the crowd from breaking the windows. I enclose clipping from our local papers. Whether I get a prize or not, I feel *I am amply repaid for the trouble and expense to which I have been put by the fine general advertisement the window has given me.* Still, of course, there is a pardonable desire to be one of the lucky ones in the contest. Trusting the display will continue to open up this new avenue of business to both of us."

The practical results of an experiment are what tell the story. Mr. Stewart's results demonstrate his experiment as a most successful one and his choice of subject a wise one. He wrote us after the display was over, as follows : " Business was splendid while the display was in the window; my daily cash sales average 25 per cent. more than ever before at the same season. It was the first display here in this section of this city, and it attracted a crowd around the window every day while it lasted. Being on the corner, and a good 25-candle-power electric bulb above it, at night it was very attractive and looked splendid. I use electricity in the store and use 25 C. P. lamps in the window, so the room is bright."

" Daily cash sales 25 % more " is just what every druggist desires and what many may have if they work for it.

DISPLAY OF MESSRS. R. B. BANCROFT & CO., NEW BRITAIN, CONN.

CHAPTER VI

Utilizing Local Features as Subjects

In other words, hit off some local event. If there is a horse-race or a foot or base-ball game in town, illustrate it with Frogs, and give them the names of the horses or the ball-players. If there is an election, let the Frogs be all voting. If any public matter is being agitated, have the Frogs holding a mass-meeting, and one Frog making a stump speech. Label some of the Frogs, if it will not give offence. Illustrate with Frogs any famous event in the old town history. If nothing better offers, let the Frogs represent some prominent and absorbing newspaper topic of the day.

Of course, there is no end to the subject for ordinary use. Frogs going a-wooing, Frogs in bathing (use real water), Frogs playing leap-frog, Frogs going to war, Frogs going to sea in tubs, etc., etc. Of these and like

ideas there is an unlimited supply, but the local hit or the timely topic is twice as enjoyable and never fails to draw greater crowds. Therefore choose a local subject.

Choose it wisely. Don't make the mistake of becoming the laughing stock of the community because of a blunder in the application. Don't secure the contempt of all by violating proprieties; choose wisely.

Several druggists who competed in our contests recognized the value of this, and hinged their displays upon some feature or occurrence happening at that time. The story of their successes is briefly told below.

One of the best instances of the use of local material we ever saw is the experience of Mr. H. G. Peters, of Youngstown, O. Mr. Peters embodied several first-class local hits in the same display, and the result can be easily seen from the description of his window. In the left of his window he has what he calls the "Frogs' Picnic." In the middle there is a pond surrounded by moss and grass. "The big Father Frog standing in the rear on

DISPLAY OF MR. S. C. ABELL, PHILADELPHIA.

the mossy bank with umbrella over him is Master of Ceremonies, while the numerous Frogs on the bank are playing leap-frog, etc. Others are still coming out of the pond to join in the festivities. A crescent moon hangs above, thus suggesting the idea that this is a moonlight scene. The silent spectators in the rear of the pond keep guard while the fun goes on. A fence of ice boxes entirely surrounds the enclosure. Right in the centre of the window is a local hit. This is labeled 'John Renner's Chickens Come Home to Roost.' John Renner is a prominent brewer in that town. He had a lot of fine fancy chickens, forty of which were stolen in one night. The police were promptly informed. The following night twenty-five were returned to the roost; the thieves were captured and brought before the Mayor. The court sentenced and sent them over the road, while the daily papers were full of it and everybody was talking about Renner's chickens. We set up a fence consisting of two uprights and two long cross bars and perched a lot of your hens and roosters on the same and so by illustrating the favored topic of the hour, we caused lots of fun and comment. On the extreme right of the win-

dow is another local hit labeled 'Starkweather's Menagerie.' Starkweather has a meat market and oyster house in Youngstown. He keeps three pet bears, a few cats, etc., which he delights to exhibit to his customers. Our Starkweather Menagerie was a collection of all kinds of animals and curiosities which you had sent to us as part of the advertising. We made a ring for these, putting them all inside it and built around them a fence out of boxes of 'Frog in your Throat?' Everybody saw the joke and enjoyed it, and, best of all, talked to everybody else about it. Several prominent ladies said they came downtown especially to see the display and pronounced it 'the cutest window they ever saw.' It was always crowded around the window, and frequently the crowd blocked the sidewalk. I got permission of the gentlemen to use their names in the exhibit, and altogether it was pronounced a great show. Yours respectfully, H. G. Peters. P. S.—Francis Murphy was conducting a series of temperance meetings here and one evening suffered from hoarseness which he attributed to 'Frog in your Throat?' 'The complaint, not the remedy.' The next day I mailed him a box of your lozenges with my compliments."

DISPLAY OF MR. S. C. YEOMANS, CHICAGO.

Everybody appreciates the taking-off of something they are perfectly familiar with, much more than simply an abstract subject. A window burlesque of some familiar local feature will never fail to attract universal attention, even though crudely prepared.

Visiting amusement enterprises can be made the fruitful subjects for very taking displays. To what extent can be seen from the experience of Mr. S. C. Yeomans, of Chicago, who made a window display upon the subject of "Frank Hall's English Winter Circus and German Water Carnival." He selected this subject because it happened just then that Frank Hall's Circus was playing to crowded houses in the Panorama Building, Wabash Avenue and Hubbard Street, Chicago. There is a large amphitheatre which is made to take up all the middle of the window. This encloses a sawdust ring on the right, and the aquarium on the left. The amphitheatre is made of boxes of "Frog in your Throat?" rising row above row, giving the Frog spectators a good view of the acrobatic skeletons performing on the horizontal bars, tight-rope walkers, daring horseback riders (monkeys on Frogs), etc. He writes: "In the aquarium, which is well stocked with goldfish, are the snails wandering

around watching the turtles, goldfish, etc. On the left, towards the front, in the grass, is 'Grover' fishing at 'Buzzard's Bay.' He seems to be having success, too, as the Mexican jumping bean tied on the line, just above the water, keeps his line moving. In the centres of the sawdust ring and the aquarium are the 'centre-poles,' over which is stretched the tight rope, upon which the 'daring Professor Bull' gives 'hourly shows.' In the sawdust ring is the ring master, whip in hand, urging on the horseback riders (monkeys riding Frogs) to do their best. We made a liberal use of the various signs on the windows, etc. The display caused a great deal of comment in this locality, and frequently during the evening the sidewalk was completely blocked with people, although I am 3½ miles from the business centre. The sale of 'Frogs,' considering the pleasant weather we have been having, is certainly phenomenal, and the future of the season looks bright for a greater business in this department."

You see the drawing effect of a local hit, even to a druggist over three miles from the business centre.

Another instance comes from Tiffin, O., where Messrs. J. W. Marquardt & Son burlesqued the Fourth

DISPLAY OF MR. F. E. JACOBSON, BETHLEHEM, PA.

Annual Poultry Show, at that time in progress in their city. Other druggists may secure a good idea of their method from this letter, as follows : " The subject of our display is a Frog-pond. This embraces many other things, among them being a Frog singing-school on a log of natural wood—burlesque on our ' Fourth Annual Poultry Show,' just at present in progress in our city. We used your roosters and made the exhibit in the cabinet, using Frogs for judges. Indoor base-ball game, now very popular in our city, the players being the Frog Nine. Exhibit of living Frogs in a glass aquarium ; two in number, each weighing nearly three pounds. Old man fishing for Frogs with flannel bait. Cabinet containing stock of ' Frog in your Throat ?' making a good display of the goods. A rockery, having ferns growing in the crevices, an old moss-covered log at base of same near the edge of the water, the water being represented by large beveled-plate mirrors ; a natural picket fence bearing signs of ' Frog in your Throat ?,' water-lilies, ferns, grasses, cat-tails, reeds, etc., growing in and near the water, cranes, water-wiens, your small birds, etc ; outside, the display of your signs and a guide-board to ' Frog in your Throat ?' pond. We received two newspaper notices of this show and also devoted the space we

owned in those two papers, about six inches square, to a special advertisement of ' Frog in your Throat ?' while the display was on."

Messrs. Marquardt & Sons' supplementary letter, concerning the results of their display, is most interesting, as one can see from it the business force which abides in the idea under discussion. From their letter written to us after the display was over, we reproduce the following extract : " Marked improvement ; consider it a splendid card. Received some very complimentary notices free. Our display proved a capital investment in bringing extra trade and causing our store to be talked about and complimented in the highest terms. Best wishes for ' Frog in your Throat ?' "

Mr. Charles F. Haas, of Canal Dover, O., took advantage of the popular excitement in his section over the proposed ship canal. In writing of his display, he says : " The ship canal from Lake Erie to the Ohio River is stirring the people here, so I had a canal made of tin. In it I placed a full-rigged boat manned by Frogs. The masts were covered with small Frogs in all positions. In the stern, a large Frog was at the helm and under an umbrella. In front, the captain was looking out through his spy-glass. Above the canal I placed the label, ' Even

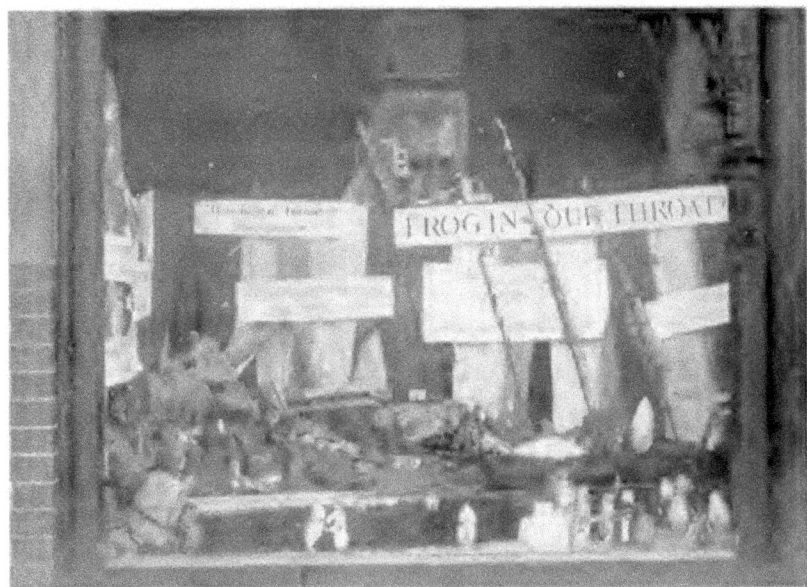

DISPLAY OF MR. CHARLES F. HAAS, CANAL DOVER, OHIO.

in Frogdom they have Ship Canals.' Besides the ship, there were on the canal numerous small boats with Frogs rowing. In front of the canal was a valley made of sawdust and colored green to resemble grass. Here under an umbrella, on a 'throne' made of a cigar box and cotton, with two small chairs, sat the King and Queen. On each side stood a guard with his bow and arrow. In front the musicians played. Before them the two gymnasts sent me were in the act of swinging on the bars. Around sat the court labeled ' King Frog enjoys a holiday.' In another part of the valley two Frogs are in the act of boxing, their gloves being made of cotton wrapped around their hands. There is also a Frog holding a small shirt on the ground. Below is a washtub. This is labeled 'Wash-day.' On the other side of the canal, we have a hill made of sand and furnace cinder. On the top of this is a coal bank with an incline railroad from it to the canal. The railroad is made of copper wire with wooden toothpicks as cross ties. Going up this railroad is a mule (driven by a Frog) drawing two empty ' coal cars.' On the canal bank, one large Frog is taking a small one a riding in a wheelbarrow. A road runs down the hill from its top, where a few miniature houses stand. Along the road are trees with owls sitting on them. There is artificial moss between the rocks. On the other side of the ' bank ' we have a 'forest,' and here the

rabbits, owls, etc., are abundant. I have a fortress made of cinder guarding the canal. Here I have placed toy cannons with Frogs as gunners. My window is diamond-shaped, so I cannot get a good picture, but I tell you I have the crowd, and sold two gross ' Frogs' in a short time. This is only a town of 4000 people, and ' hard up ' at that. I am well pleased with the result. Understand I did not attempt to compete when I made this—didn't see your advertisement—did not read it, I mean, until I had the show made, but I'll enter just for fun."

There are towns upon towns where some enterprise similar to this is in progress. It can be just as easily adapted to a " Frog in your Throat?" display as this Ohio ship canal. If you stop and think a moment, we are very sure that possibilities like these will crowd your mind. And we have no doubt that your results will fully equal Mr. Haas', who writes as follows concerning them : " Before I made the display I had sold only a few dozen ' Frog in your Throat?' I sold nine dozen in one week, which, under the circumstances, was very good, I think. Good window displays always improve business, and I noticed a marked improvement in my business, especially in your toc line. I got several very pretty notices which did me much good, worth to me many times the cost of the display. I learned of the value of window advertis-

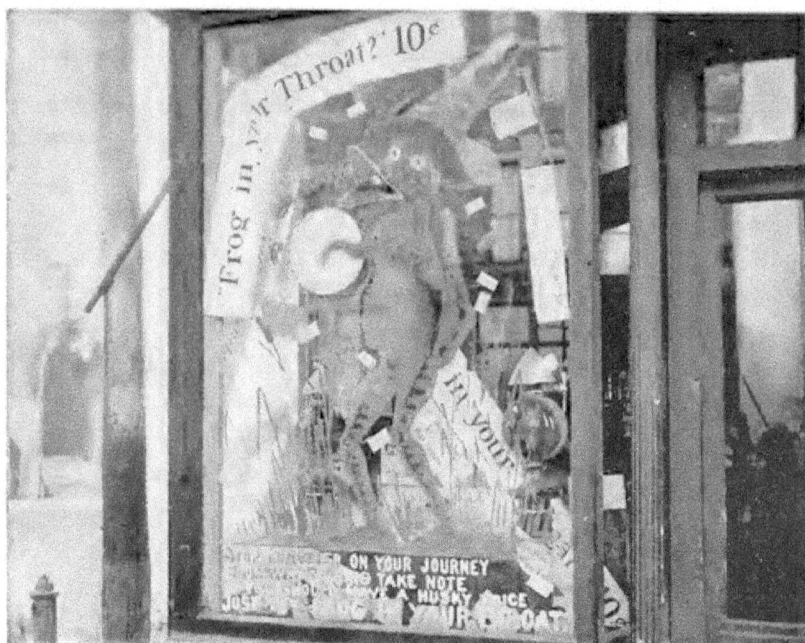

DISPLAY OF MR. T. R. ANDERSON, PORT JERVIS, N. Y.

ing before I competed for the prize, and my display was only one for the benefit of my business."

One of the newspaper notices spoken of by Mr. Haas, is as follows:

LOOK IN HIS WINDOW

"Charley Haas has his drug show window fancily fixed up for Fair folks. He has a cinder mountain with a natural tunnel; a stream of real wet water with a lake at the end; a railway with sand ballast and a train of miniature cars with locomotive. But the realest feature is a whole lot of croaking Frogs and tree-toads. You only need to squeeze their stomachs a little and they will sing for rain just like life. Charley is a wide-awake advertiser, and his window will attract much attention."
—*Iron Valley, O., Reporter.*

While a State political victory cannot be said to be local to any one town, yet its effect is felt everywhere to such an extent that any celebration of it has nearly as much force as a matter purely local. One famous gubernatorial contest in Pennsylvania was celebrated through a clever window display by Mr. F. H. Ruhl, of Manheim. Democrats may not agree with the spirit of Mr. Ruhl's display, but all will agree that the idea of taking advantage of the political situation was a bright one.

Mr. Ruhl describes his display as follows: "The display was made a day after our local election. In the front of the window, to the right, are a number of Frogs celebrating the Republican victory by a walk around. At the head of the column is one carrying a banner with '236,000 Hurrah,' plurality for Hastings at that time. To the rear of this is a lake, and at one end the 'Salt River' boat is bearing the defeated party to its destination. The boat also carries boxes of 'Frog in your Throat?' Back of this scene, perched prominently, sits a Frog fishing. Further back and to the left are two Frogs out walking under a sunshade, one carrying a baby Frog. Still further to the left is a Frog walking the tight rope, his balancing pole having a Frog lozenge at each end. There also are two Frogs performing on a trapeze. One large Frog to the extreme left is playing the street hand-organ, with a monkey perched on the organ. Herewith I send you copies of our two local papers containing notices of my show. One thing above all others shows how my 'Frog in your Throat?' advertisements paid me; during the winter before I sold five or six dozen: last winter sold three gross." Here's a window at work.

CHAPTER VII

Utilizing Animate Nature or Mechanical Movement

This is one of the most important subjects in this series, for in the matters discussed in it lie the highest possibilities of remunerative window display. There is a vast difference between an ordinary "pretty" display and an ingenious one—one containing a mechanical counterfeit of some form of life.

Think a moment! A pool of water is ordinarily a most uninteresting object, but *introduce it into your store window*, with scenic backgrounds, and it will draw crowds from morning till night. Advance one step further and let it be moving water (as a running stream or rapids, or a waterfall, or a mill race), and your window will be the talk of the town.

Another form of animate nature is animal life. Now a turtle is about the dullest of animate things, but see him in a store window and he will, by his very unusual presence, arouse quite a stir. It is surprising how exciting to the average beholder is almost any living creature in a store window. Of course it is not always convenient to secure real life, nor is it always necessary.

Then consider the great range of mechanical moving objects. Any toy store can supply the machinery for such a display. If no toy store is at hand, try the watch-repairer's ingenuity at contriving some simple form of "wound up" mechanism. Clothe this mechanism to suit your fancy. A swinging pendulum may be converted into a miniature swing with a Frog sitting in the seat. A slowly-revolving-wheel may easily be the motive power of a paper or pasteboard windmill. A small toy balloon held captive, can support a string of acrobatic Frogs, and the moving air will sway them gently to and fro. (To aid you in giving life to the window, we have, as many know, manufactured a large number of automatic figures. They jump, they bow, they drink, they exercise in full view of delighted crowds. Many have used them, more could do so with profit.)

A large number who competed in our most recent window display were wise in their generation and took advantage of these facts. The results which their efforts elicited, far more eloquently than words of ours, tell whether our statements are founded on fact. One of these firms was Turner & Kantner, of Altoona, Pa. The movement used in their display was very simple—merely a stream of running water—but it drew the crowds. It makes no difference how simple it is, if it embodies a moving effect, it will attract the eye and do the work.

DISPLAY OF MR. W. G. TOPLIS, GERMANTOWN, PA

DISPLAY OF MR. JAMES M. DISQUE, COVINGTON, KY.

The bottom of Turner & Kantner's window was covered with moss; and in the centre was placed a mound of stones with clinging moss and growing ferns. A stream of real water made three falls over the stones into the miniature lake below, in which small Frogs were sitting on leaves, etc., and large Frogs on the bank fishing. To the left, on a raised mound, was a Frog orchestra, with leader, holding raised stick in one hand, and " In Old Madrid " in the other. On the right, the Altoona Football Team was lined up ready for play. There is a Frog on top of the goal, directly to the rear. Each Frog bears the name of a player, and it attracted a great deal of attention. Referee and umpire were there on either side.

Further to the right of the football show, was arranged a poultry yard.

A burnt child dreads the fire, but one comfortably warmed by it will return to it again. Turner & Kantner wrote to us that they intended competing in our next display; they will then find this experience a great advantage. For their last display they state : " We noticed a general improvement in business during our display, and received several very nice notices from the local press. Would like to compete again if you get up another contest. We can say that during our display we enjoyed a vastly increased business in ' Frog in your Throat ?' "

There is a scope in that expression, " vastly increased

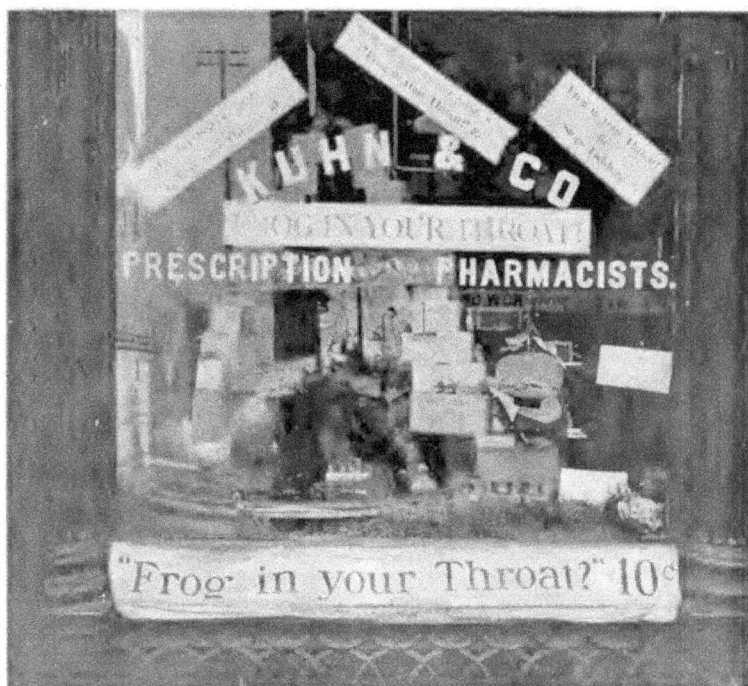

DISPLAY OF MESSRS. KUHN & CO., OMAHA, NEB.

business, which nothing short of careful window-display advertising can adequately cover.

Messrs. Kuhn & Co., of Omaha, Neb., made one of the most elaborate mechanical displays of the contest. It must have cost them considerable money to make a display like the one whose description follows, but we doubt not they are fully satisfied. Their statement regarding the crowd-drawing feature of their display is pretty good evidence of that.

Kuhn & Co. used as their background a gigantic arch built out of the wooden gross boxes and the dozen box packages of "Frog in your Throat?" Under this arch is a "mountain" built of piled-up rocks and covered with moss, grass, small plants, etc. Around this mountain is a railroad track entering the mountain by a tunnel at one side. The ground work of this mountain is real earth over which was laid grass sod. This was sprinkled every day and thus kept bright and green. The mountain was then built up with earth and rocks, the tunnel being carefully cleft through it. A miniature track was laid, 6 inches in width, with crushed stone for ballast. Upon this track

was run a steam locomotive with tender and two coaches and a Frog for engineer and brakeman. This locomotive would run after being fired up (with alcohol) about 25 minutes, the steam escaping through the stack, having all the appearance of smoke. There, at the rocky top of the mountain, came a stream of water constantly running down its side into a circular pond near the corner iron post. In this pond were goldfish. Over it a bridge was thrown, upon which a train of cars run. At the entrance to the tunnel was the depot, upon the platform of which stood a monkey with a grip wearing a high hat. Around it was the label, "Agent for 'Frog in your Throat?'" Through the fields were various animals, while up the sides of the mountain innumerable Frogs were climbing higher and higher.

The effect which a display like this would have upon an average public, filled as it was with animated miniature life, is indescribable. If any druggist-reader of these articles doubts its efficacy, let him follow Messrs. Kuhn & Co.'s ideas in his own town. In closing their own description of the display, the firm state—

DISPLAY OF MR. JOHN BRITTAIN, ALLEGHENY, PA.

*"Crowds were around this window continually.
When we wanted a crowd, we could always get a large
one by setting that train in motion."*

A crowd around a drugstore window that don't mean
dollars in that druggist's till, does mean an excessively
slow druggist.

A window display which draws a crowd so large that
a policeman interferes, is hardly a failure, do you think?
That was exactly the case with Mr. John Brittain, of
Allegheny, Pa. Mr. Brittain utilized a well known
Pennsylvania feature—an oil well—but notwithstanding
the familiarity of the people with it, it succeeded amaz-
ingly. Mr. Brittain's own description of his display is
good enough to reproduce verbatim—

"The most essential part of this display," he says, "is
the miniature oil-well in full operation, situated on the
top of a mound built up of moss. The motive power used
in the operation of the oil-well is derived from a small
water motor situated in a shed placed to the left of the
derrick. By means of a belt from the motor a flywheel is
operated, which in turn operates the walking beam, giving
it the motion universally used in drilling for oil or gas.
The driller, which is a small Frog, stands in his place at
the drill. By a mechanical contrivance, the Frog is given
the motion of twisting the drill, usually the duty of the
driller. By means of a combination of strings, fastened
to the drill end of walking-beam, and then to a Frog
situated on the extreme top of the derrick, at each motion

DISPLAY OF MR. PAUL G. HEINEMANN, CHICAGO.

of the beam the strings are tightened, making the Frog go through a series of gymnastic exercises. The exhaust water, that is, the water after having passed through the water motor, is utilized in a way so as to form a small stream, of which a host of small Frogs and ducks have taken possession. The mound, which represents the side of a hill, is covered with moss, trees and flowers, the whole presenting a neat and attractive appearance."

Mr. Brittain adds, concerning the attention drawn by his display—"Our display attracted such large crowds that the policeman asked me if he should make the crowd move away from the window. We told him that we had placed it there to draw a crowd."

Some druggists would pooh pooh the idea of there being any business value in a crowd like this. "Pshaw! They wouldn't buy anything!" they would exclaim. Well, if some of them wouldn't buy something, it's the druggist's own fault. A druggist who couldn't sell goods through a crowd that necessitated a policeman's services, when that crowd was drawn by his own window, is a pretty poor druggist.

A reproduction of some form of nature is always interesting, more especially when it contains some movable feature, mechanical or otherwise. One of the prettiest ideas of this sort was conceived by Messrs. Federman & Haller, Kansas City, Mo. The scene represented in their display is a typical Frog pond. The bottom of the window is covered with a tin pan 5 feet by 6 feet, the bottom of the pan being covered with sand and then filled with water. Around this, covering up the edges, are rocks, back of which is built a cliff. The top of the cliff is a typical log cabin, in which can be seen evidences of its being inhabited. A rubber tube is attached to a steam radiator and the steam allowed to escape through the chimney of the cabin, representing smoke. Through crevices in the cliff there was arranged, by rubber tubing, attached to the hydrant, a stream of water, which is constantly running down the cliff, over the rocks and into the pond below, which is stocked with goldfish. The rocks, cliff and miniature lake form an excellent background for the placing of the Frogs, snakes and other paraphernalia.

This is exceedingly simple, you see. Simply two rubber tubes, one for steam and the other for water, and to the display is lent a natural charm which stationary exhibits never possess. Every mechanical display made in our contest drew a crowd so large it blocked the street. Listen to what Federman & Haller say about their crowd— "Whether we draw a prize or not, we feel *we have gained the desired result* in drawing to our window crowds of people from morning till night. The longer the display remains, the bigger the crowd seems to grow and the greater the increase in the sale of 'Frog in your Throat?'"

A firm progressive enough to incept a display like this is always wise enough to understand that when the crowd is once before a druggist's window, the amount of money they leave in the store rests with the druggist.

It takes an unusual ingenuity to devise a display as elaborate as the one made by Mr. James M. Disque, of Covington, Ky. The background for this display Mr. Disque had painted especially for the occasion, and he spent considerable money on it in other ways. His experience shows that while expensive elaboration is not in the least essential to a successful window display, it is, nevertheless, politic to spend money when you feel able.

Mr. Disque made two displays. The first was similar to the second, only there was no movement connected with it. The stationary display was in the window but a short time, the results not being as large as Mr. Disque thought warranted. Read carefully what he says about the results of his second display—

"The most prominent feature in the display was the Frogs coasting down the street and on down the hill to the lake. There were never less than four sleds with Frogs on them in view at one time, continually moving down the coasting track and returning underneath the display to the top of the hill, the power being supplied by a small motor. The largest sled had four Frogs and a box of 'Frog in your Throat?' on it. Another sled had a dog and a Frog. All the other sleds had one Frog on them each. In one place it represented a Frog having fallen off the sled and rolling down the hill. In the painted background of the display was a representation of a house on fire, and the fire department at work trying to save the building, the entire crew being composed of Frogs, with their engine at the lake pumping, and a 'Frog in your Throat?' advertisement sign coming out of the chimney to represent smoke. Also the Frogs carrying and pulling two lines of hose up the hill, and Frog firemen on their ladders going up to fight the flames. You will also notice one Frog fireman going up the ladder with an axe on his shoulder. At the top of the hill on the left there is the ladder-wagon, with a Frog driver and a Frog steersman, and a 'Frog in your Throat?' sign on the wagon. You will also notice what is intended for the chief driving up the hill in his cart with a banner of 'Frog in your Throat?' flying from the end of his whip, he blowing a horn on his way to the fire. On the hillside you will see the trees growing here and there. These have owls and other birds sitting on

them. There are also two roosters fighting over a box of 'Frog in your Throat?' and some Frogs shown snow-balling the coasters. In the lake you will notice a vessel drawn up alongside the wharf unloading its cargo of 'Frog in your Throat?'"

If we were to make any criticism of this display, it would be that Mr. Disque gave people rather too much for their money. It is never well to overload a window display with too many incidents. We admit the absurdity of "argyin' agin' a success," as Josh Billings says, and Mr. Disque's results certainly seem to point in that direction. In the letter which accompanied the photos of his display he wrote— "My window display of 'Frog in your Throat?' was the means of selling for me more of your goods during the four weeks of this display than I sold all of last season." It is well to reflect right here that Mr. Disque's profit was 100 per cent. We furnished the goods and the advertising matter, Mr. Disque supplied the window, and acted as broker at 100 per cent commission.

"Dollars in our pocket" is the magic, cheerful phrase into which the J. F. Bomm Drug Co., of Evansville, Ind., condense the results of their display. This firm utilized electricity as a motive power for the mechanical devices in their window. The platform of the window was covered with green grass. To the left was a Ferris wheel and to the right a merry-go-round. Both had their seats filled with Frogs and both were run by a small electric motor. A lake, 2 feet by 5 feet long, occupied the centre of the window. In the lake was a fountain throwing a small stream 2 feet high. The lake was stocked with small fish. The window was topped off by a large Japanese umbrella, and for a background they had Japanese panels, 'Frog in your Throat?' signs and plants, a small statue of Liberty, rocks, fossils, miniature tree of bunched coral, etc. The window was on exhibition one month. It was well lighted day and night. The firm's letter to us regarding the display contains a paragraph as follows— "Crowds blocked the sidewalk in front continually. It proved to be an excellent advertisement for 'Frog in your Throat?' which has shown increased sales week after week."

Beside the display in his window, Mr. Bomm also made a very effective and pretty display inside his store by the means of Frogs, plants, cut-outs, Japanese panels, etc.

The Bomm Co.'s report of the results of this display, made in writing to us, was short, terse, and straight to the point— "It stimulated general trade," they say, "and made a demand for 'Frog in your Throat?,' our store popular, and dollars in our pocket."

It's a happy druggist who can gain all of these things with one window display.

Mr. Paul G. Heinemann, of Chicago, Ill., took as much pains with his displays as any druggist competing. He cleaned out his show windows and changed them every Saturday. The crowd would collect every time,

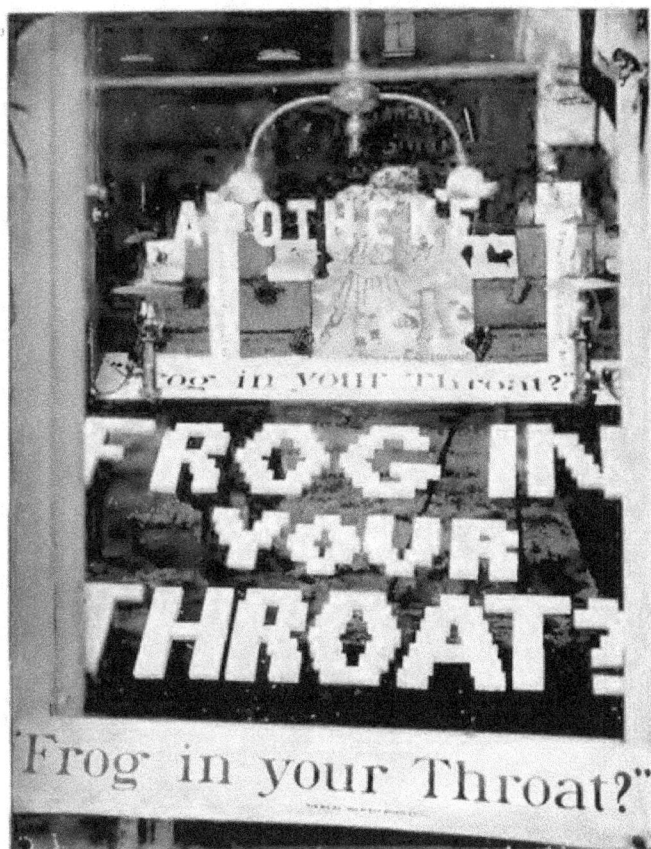

DISPLAY OF MR. GEORGE LAMPING, MERIDEN, CONN.

he says, to see what the new show was going to be. Some of the ideas worked into Mr. Heinemann's shows were a baseball team of Frogs in full swing, a toboggan-slide, a fine Ferris wheel, the cars being dozen boxes of "Frog in your Throat?," a full-rigged sloop with "Frog in your Throat?" printed on all the sails. There also is a merry-go-round, showing numerous Frogs at play. This merry-go-round and the Ferris wheel were kept turning all day long by means of a water-wheel, which was made in the sink close by.

Mr. Heinemann's testimony about his display is as follows—"The whole thing was rather an expensive arrangement, but the turning wheel drew crowds of people around my window at all hours of the day. Am certain of considerable improvement in business. My store is comparatively new (only 2½ years), and business has steadily improved. Part of this is undoubtedly due to judicious window advertising, among which 'Frog in your Throat?' was the most conspicuous, and drew considerable attention; so much so, that my neighbors here had the impression that I was the special agent for these goods."

DISPLAY OF KAERCHER'S PHARMACY, ALLEGHENY, PA.

CHAPTER VIII

The Value of Ingenuity

One of the most valuable factors in the making of a successful window display—one that will draw the attention, and not merely be regarded as "pretty," is ingenuity. In every case where a druggist takes time to lay out a plan of his display, giving it as many *points* as possible, it will attract the attention of ten persons to every one who will stop to gaze upon a window filled with a quantity of pretty things, aimlessly arranged and possessing no ingenuity whatever.

Has it occurred to you that twenty-five cents' worth of cotton wool will make a winter scene in your whole window? Glass is only another name for imitation ice.

Let Frogs skate, snowball each other, coast, etc. Here is one idea.

In just this way you can think of a dozen possibilities. Frogs are great acrobats, and this suggests tight-rope walking, trapeze work, handsprings, somersaults.

Go to a toy store for a fine line of ideas. Here is a toy-wagon, hitch Frogs to it, and put a Frog as driver, with boxes of "Frog in your Throat?" in the wagon. Here is a big doll; reproduce the story of Gulliver's Travels, and use the Frogs as Lilliputians, with the doll as Brobdignag. Or get a toy sailboat, and float it in a basin, with Frogs as sailors.

Caricature the "Twentieth Century Woman" Have a football game or a cake-walk. In general, use ingenuity. Talk it over with your friends. They will suggest many things you have never thought of. Read the

DISPLAY OF MESSRS. STEVENS & MANNING, BOUND BROOK, N. J.

papers for late events. You will find that there is no subject which cannot be treated. Frogs adapt themselves to almost every need. There is no other article in the whole range of a druggist's stock that is so endlessly capable of window displays as "Frog in your Throat?" Only use ingenuity and work with the brain as well as the hands.

Some druggists who participated in our 1895 contest contented themselves with merely filling their windows with material. They didn't care how it was arranged, they hadn't time possibly to lay out an ingenious display possessing some meaning. Others were wise in their generation and reaped large reward for every minute spent in devising ingenious effects.

Mr. A. J. Kaercher, of Allegheny, Pa., was one of the latter class, and you can't convince him that window display does not pay, by a month's steady argument. The first prize in the contest was awarded to Mr. A. J. Kaercher, and he displayed a zeal in this connection which was second to none. He may be said, as a matter of fact, to have made six displays, having made such alterations

on six different occasions during the time the display was in his window as to amount to making a new one each time. Mr. Kaercher's first display was made in a fine large window, on a corner, having a plate-glass frontage to each of two streets.

The great idea of this window was a revolving Christmas Tree. A 9-feet pine tree was fixed on a 5-feet revolving stand, run by a small steam-engine. This tree was covered with toys, consisting of holiday novelties, Frogs, Japanese toys, etc., and brilliantly lighted up by no less than 33 colored electric lights; these lights changing color every fifteen seconds. The revolving base on which this "Christmas Tree" stood was covered over with a mound of moss, on which were Frogs, etc. Around the circumference of this were arranged 27 dozen boxes of "Frog in your Throat?"

In the front corner of the window it will be noticed that there are two miniature fountains with swimming swans, etc. These were kept flowing with real water all day long. In the background may be seen a large screen with the words "Frog in your Throat?" and a picture of

DISPLAY OF MR. JACKSON.

the two children taken from our own cut-out, which was standing on the floor of the window, underneath the right-hand side of the Christmas Tree.

Mr. Kaercher took this cut-out and had it redrawn in colors, five times the size of the original, to form a background to his display.

In writing to us of the results of his displays he says : " I cheerfully acknowledge that I was very agreeably surprised at the result of your great " Frog in your Throat ? " display success, and sincerely hope that the sales of your valuable preparation will continue in the future as they have in the past."

If we had a dollar for every druggist who was " agreeably surprised " at the results of a good " Frog in your Throat ? " window display, we should have a comfortable little pile of filthy lucre.

An exceeding curious and ingenious display was made by Mr. S. C. Abell, of Philadelphia. This display must have cost Mr. Abell a great deal of thought, but he is our authority for the statement that it captured the whole public by storm. This is Mr. Abell's own description of his very striking display : " This display was the admiration and wonderment of hundreds of people who were

attracted by the great orginality and by the awe-inspiring appearance of a full-sized skeleton, which stood in the centre of the window, represented as just rising from the grave, its feet resting on a large tombstone, which was made of a number of boxes of ' Frog in your Throat ? ' In his right hand he holds a large sign bearing the following words in large letters : ' Clear your voice or come to this.' The left arm is held aloft, bidding every one take warning and avoid the condition to which he is reduced by not taking ' Frog in your Throat ? ' In the mouth of the skeleton is a large Frog. In the throat are a number of smaller ones, and all over the bones are a number of Frogs crawling towards the throat with signs, ' We are making for the Throat.' The eyes of the skeleton, as well as those of the Frog in his mouth, are lighted up with small incandescent lights by means of storage batteries, which make a very brilliant effect in the evening. The bottom and sides of the window were covered with moss, and in front was a lake, with a fountain in the centre, which was constantly playing, and on the bank of the lake were innumerable Frogs in the act of jumping into the water. In the lake were a dozen live Frogs, a turtle, some goldfish, which could be seen con-

DISPLAY OF E. L. GRAHAM, MUSCATINE, IA.

stantly going through their respective antics. The lake was represented as situated on an elevated plateau; the hills gradually sloping down towards the plate glass. Along the upper bank of the lake was a high road laid out with small trees and an iron fence winding all along the road. One end of this road emerged from a tunnel in the hill-side, and extended along the entire length of the window, on the banks of the lake, becoming lost to view at the extreme far end, where it disappeared among the evergreen trees. Traveling along the road was a cart laden with 'Frog in your Throat!' On the cart were displayed signs as follows: 'From Hance Brothers & White to Abell's Pharmacy.'

"Immediately back of the skeleton, and midway between the two elevated points of the large tombstone (which can be seen in the picture), was a smaller tombstone, over which was suspended an enormously large Frog, kindly lent to us by your representative. All over the window the Frogs were hopping around, bearing the signs, 'Frog in your Throat?' The background was made of palms, ferns and evergreen trees; with green cloth in some places to represent a forest. Along the

back were also suspended your various signs about 'Frog in your Throat?' In the branches of the trees were birds of different kinds singing the praises of 'Frog in your Throat?' Right across the top of the window was the large muslin sign. A sign on the corner of the window bearing the letters, 'Take Warning,' impressed everyone with the dire necessity of 'Stopping that tickling' with 'Frog in your Throat?'"

The happy results of Mr. Abell's ingenious display forms one of our strongest arguments for the bestowal of care upon such a fruitful matter as a window display. In his own words, these are as follow: "Our business was increased about one-third above the general run of daily sales. Our window display was the talk of the neighborhood, and we were complimented on the originality of the design, and the multitude were loud in the praises of 'Frog in your Throat?'"

Now, if Mr. Abell had simply thrown together a "pretty" display, his neighbors would have looked at it, possibly admired it for a moment, and—forgotten all about it. Mr. Abell would have saved time in preparing his display, but he would have lost heavily in unsecured results.

DISPLAY OF MESSRS. W. D. MATHIS & CO., SALT LAKE CITY, UTAH.

The display of Messrs. Daugherty Bros., of Jeannette, Pa., is worthy of mention in this connection : for it is one of the most elaborate ones of the entire contest. According to a paper published in the town, Daugherty Bros.' " Frog in your Throat ?" window display was the most novel and attracted more attention than any other window ever arranged in Jeannette. It was a whole show in itself and a jolly crowd could always be found around it. The window was arranged to represent a mountain scene. In the centre of the window was a lake of water around an old castle and the lake was stocked with a number of goldfish, which some Frogs along the bank were trying to catch with a hook and line. From one corner of the window came a little pebbled run which emptied into the lake. St. Patrick was at one end of the scene on a mountain of rocks driving out the snakes which appear at every crevice. At the other end was a pious-looking Frog on a large rock, with a dime in one hand and a box of " Frog in your Throat ?" in the other, preaching to a large congregation of Frogs on the moss below. In the back of the window was a small railway train laden with " Frog in your Throat ?" which the Frogs were busy unloading and carrying into a fac-simile of Daugherty's drugstore. Other noticeable features of

the window are the race of the monkeys and Frogs, frog-band, cat-fight, the devil, parrots, monkeys, storks, etc. The window was well worth a trip to see as the crowds in front showed.

We wrote to Messrs. Daugherty Bros. as to their success with the display, and received the following reply :

Dear Sirs : I was away from home on a little vacation when yours of recent date was received, which will explain its not being answered earlier. Replying to same, would say that we were very agreeably surprised at the result our window display had on trade in general, and " Frog in your Throat ?" in particular. The average sale of " Frog in your Throat ?" was over a dozen boxes a day during the display, our best day being over two dozen. We are more than pleased with this, our first attempt, and will be glad to take part in any contest you may arrange in the future.

Respectfully yours,
DAUGHERTY BROS.
S. C. D.

Another firm " agreeably surprised " at their harvest. From this statement's frequent recurrence it would seem as if there had been a universal idea on druggists' part that window display amounted to but little. The rapid increase of the use of window advertising in the last few years tells whether the idea was correct or not.

Mr. Louis Marnitz, of Chicago, made a display which

DISPLAY OF KAERCHER'S PHARMACY, ALLEGHENY, PA.

certainly entitled him to a prize for ingenuity. Taking his display as a whole, it was a simple affair, but it had an *idea* and a *point* in it. That is what a window display must have to succeed as it should and can.

The subject of Mr. Marnitz's was a battle between the "Frog in your Throat?" army and the Husky Voices army. The battle ground was the floor of the window. One of the armies consisted of skeletons and other ugly and monstrous creatures. This was the army of the Husky Voices intended to typify coughs, colds, and all throat troubles. The other army consisted of Frogs and typified the lozenge, which is recommended as able to conquer these dire troubles. The Frogs were shown advancing on the other army, beating them down with swords, spears, etc., thus typifying the victory of "Frog in your Throat?" This window was lighted up with numerous Japanese lanterns in each of which candles were kept burning every evening from six to eleven. The battle was witnessed by crowds of smiling faces.

When the druggist making the display is himself enthusiastic over its success, it is pretty safe to conclude that it *was* a success. Mr. Marnitz says of his display, "I am very glad to state that our business during the exhibit, and since then, has improved wonderfully, for we have now moved into a more spacious and more prominent corner store. I will most certainly compete again if you get up another contest."

CHAPTER IX

Individuality

There is no factor more potent in bringing to a merchant an ever-increasing amount of trade than a striking, but at the same time attractive individuality. Emphasis may as well be put on the latter as on the former, for every town has its most untidy store and its most cross-grained merchant. It is needless to say that an individuality of this sort is not a money-maker. But given an individuality that is attractive, and withal striking, and results are sure to follow. Where can a profitable individuality be so strongly and so widely impressed upon the greatest number of possible buyers as through your show-window? Indeed, how can one call attention to any quality of one's business so well as through this medium?

Individuality is the true essence of advertising. Every advertiser who has achieved a large degree of success has been one who worked outside of the beaten lines.

Advertising is of two sorts ; that which costs somebody time and money, and that which comes for nothing, and the secret of the success of the individual advertiser is that his paid-for advertising is backed up by a vast amount of curiosity as to what will be the next move, when it will occur, and descriptions to those who have not seen the last brilliant thing by those who have

DISPLAY OF MR. GEORGE D. COOK, ANDERSON, IND.

The druggists who have been skeptical as to the value of the crowds of the curious and the talk occasioned by the striking window display should learn a lesson from that prince of advertisers, the late P. T. Barnum, who, in response to a bitter attack made upon him by one of the New York papers, said, "I don't care what they say about me: when I do care is when they say nothing about me."

There is positive commercial value in "talk" and popular interest, provided there is a merchant who is able to take advantage of it. Such a man is Mr. John B. Edie, of McKeesport, Pa., who believes in getting out of the rut and calling attention to himself and to his store in a way that will not be denied. Although Mr. Edie spent several hundred dollars in preparing his display, he writes to us as follows:

"Increase in general business 25%. Who asks does this pay?"

It is a great thing to increase business 25%. Almost any drugstore without adding to its selling force, its items of light, rent, heat, could take care of 25% more business very comfortably—if it could get it—and it can. This would mean very much more than 25% additional profit. Figure it out for yourself and see if it is not so.

But to return to Mr. Edie. His *piece de resistance* was described by his local paper in the following manner: "A very attractive feature of this season is the beautiful window gotten up in the interest of that

famous cough lozenge "Frog in your Throat?" by Mr. John B. Edie. This window is a work of art, and attracts hundreds of passers-by. It is recognized as a perfect model of the landscape gardening and colonnade, which was situated between the two French buildings at the World's Fair. The whole effect is the same as that made by the staff used in the construction of World's Fair buildings. The fountain (which is really a series of fountains) is supplied by Frogs throwing water from their mouths to the highest fountain, which runs over each of the series of steps. The steps lead from the lawn to the colonnade, which is inhabited by Frogs and 'Frog in your Throat?' boxes. Mr. Edie won third prize by his window display last year, and this window bids fair for the banner prize. Another attraction, which makes it more beautiful at night, is the thirty electric lights burning throughout the lawn and colonnade. Above the display and as a background is a sign 'Frog in your Throat?' made of 500 small Frogs."

The above paragraph is a very fair description of the general appearance of Mr. Edie's window, but it by no means does justice to this magnificent display. Some additional details are contained in Mr. Edie's letter which reads as follows: "The big display was in the window from October 30th till February 6th. We kept changing and adding to the attractions constantly. You see, good as the window was, it was not allowed to grow stale. During the entire time we had in the win-

DISPLAY OF MR. JOHN B. EDIE, McKEESPORT, PA.

dow four live Mexican frogs, which by themselves would have attracted people to the display. The bronze frogs which constituted a part of the fountain threw a steady stream of water to the highest fountain, and this dripping and running down over the series of fountains made a striking and beautiful scene. This display so completely captivated all who saw it that we constantly had a crowd before it, and all pronounced it a genuine work of art. At night with the charm of 33 electric lights it was especially beautiful.

"For three weeks during the holidays we had a 12 foot Christmas Tree in our other window, splendidly decked with Frog in your Throat? toys, yards of tinsel, ornaments, etc., and lighted with 12 electric lights, assorted tints, by an automatic drum, which switched the electric lights off and on continually. In this window we had two large statues holding electric lights."

Mr. Edie's readiness to take advantage of advertising opportunities is further demonstrated by the following: "My Frog suit worn by a man on horseback, and finely trimmed with frogs, Frog in your Throat? lanterns, and lots of red, white and blue garlands, while behind him rode my other large frog, was the centre of interest, and received the best newspaper article of all the displays in our Merchants' Caravan held here in November, in which one merchant had eight wagons laden with the most elaborate displays."

The newspaper notice referred to reads as follows: "The display of John B. Edie, the Walnut Street druggist, was probably the most novel in the parade. Mr. Edie's display was a man made up to represent a frog, which is the trade mark of Frog in your Throat? the cough medicine." "In every public event," continues Mr. Edie, "masquerades, etc., that have taken

DISPLAY OF LOWE'S PHARMACY, NEW HAVEN, CONN.

place since last October, my Frog Man has been the leading attraction."

Describing his window display campaign Mr. Edie writes: "Our first window, which was left in two weeks, was the full 10-gross lot, as you will see by photo. In this window we had a large card which read: "This window contains 1440 boxes of Frog in your Throat? the amount we sold last year. We expect to double it this year. Then after we put in our big display we moved this lot to the other window, and day after day as fast as it was sold we removed half a dozen boxes at a time, which, of course, was observed by patrons and passers-by, and greatly helped us in the sale. We are now almost out, which for a place of this size, and located off the principal street as we are, means that our plan of using the ideas and advertising matter you furnish, and a determined hustle, would sell 10 gross of Frog in your Throat? every year for three-fourths of the druggists the world over." And we believe it would.

But Mr. Edie was not through yet. He further writes: "At the curb in front of our store we have had in operation for two weeks a drinking fountain supplied from our 25-barrel tank, with the finest artesian well water, which runs through four frogs which are in an upright position. The streams flow from the Frogs mouths and strike the same place. We have supplied the fountain with several aluminum cups, and a thousand people a day drink at this fountain. Our city water is unfit for use, on account of the great amount of sulphur and acid from coal mines, which makes our Frog in your Throat? fountain the more popular, and it is talked of all over the city. It is the only street fountain ever erected here by a business man." Concerning this Mr. Edie's local newspaper speaks forth again. "John B. Edie, the popular druggist of South Walnut Street, is having erected in front of his place of business, a handsome fountain for the benefit of the thirsty public. The fountain will be filled with cold sparkling well water from Mr. Edie's drilled well. The fountain itself is a unique affair. It is an advertisement of 'Frog in your Throat?' and the water will run through the mouths of four iron frogs. Surmounting the fountain is an equestrian statue of Buffalo Bill."

Can anyone after reading all of the foregoing doubt that Mr. Edie's individuality is very strongly impressed upon the people of his town? Note that the newspaper calls him "the popular druggist of South Walnut Street." Do you not suppose that almost every time one

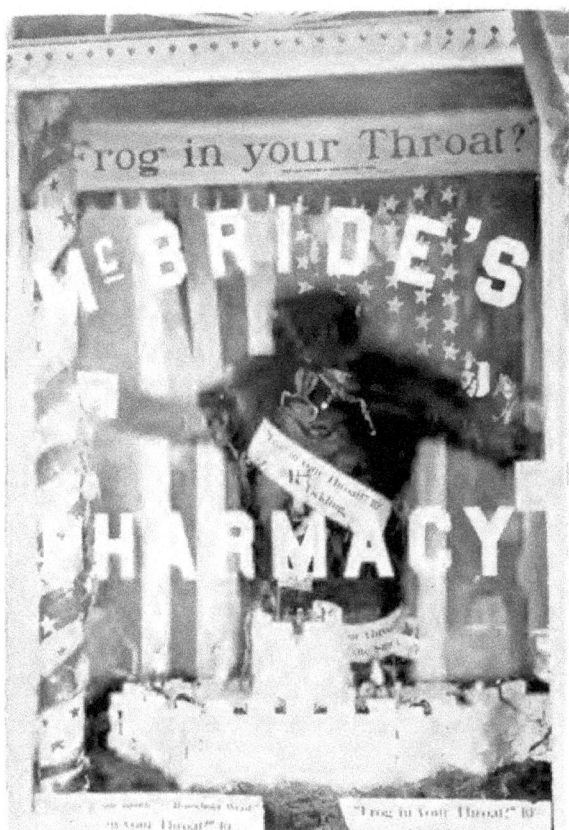

DISPLAY OF McBRIDE'S PHARMACY, KINGSTON. N. Y.

of Mr. Edie's townspeople thinks of drugs, sodas or specialties, Mr. Edie's name and the things that he has done are brought to remembrance? And how much do you suppose this is worth?

Following along in the line of Mr. Edie, another firm which has succeeded in stamping its individuality upon its townspeople, is that of Messrs. R. B. Bancroft & Co., of New Britain, Conn.

Mr. Bancroft made a window which captivated the town and which made his general business "very good" all the time that the display was in the window, and sold for him four gross of "Frog in your Throat?" in four weeks' time. To say that the window captivated the public is hardly putting it strong enough, for Mr. Bancroft writes that a policeman was frequently needed to disperse the crowd in order to make a passage way.

He describes his window as follows:

"The Brownie Frog on the window, painted in colors, holding a cat-tail with a leaf-shaped banner, 'Frog in your Throat? 10 cents,' was in itself a very striking feature and attracted the attention of the would-be-passer-by."

We are strongly tempted to sermonize on the phrase "the would-be-passer-by." Mr. Bancroft, Mr. Edie and many others have discovered that the man who will not ordinarily notice a window is not invulnerable to a thoroughly good display, and that more often than not when he refuses to look at the window it's because there's nothing there that he cares to see. Continuing, he writes:

"The bottom of the window was turfed with green moss, which grew to about five or six inches high during the display, and looked as green and nice as could be, much in contrast to the icy pavements and cold atmosphere outside. This grassy plot represented a meadow

DISPLAY OF MR. JOHN D. BLAUVELT, NYACK, N. Y.

on each side of the lake which occupied the centre of the window, and cattle, horses, sheep, etc., fed at their leisure, while here and there Frogs were playing leap-frog and other like amusements, and some were sitting placidly among the long grass, lillies and chrysanthemums, which seemed to grow in great profusion in the meadow.

"The scenery in the rear of the window extended the length of the window, and was five feet high, and repre-sented a mountain and water scene, all painted in rich coloring with trees, rocks, ferns, brooklets, etc., and same blended nicely to meet the green grass of the meadow at the bottom, as did the top to meet the blue sky above, which was made of sky-blue cheese cloth, drawn from the top of the scenery in the rear to the top of the window glass in front, and looked very natural indeed, with the clouds floating through the blue heaven.

" In the rear of the window on the left side we built up rocks of different dimensions to meet the rocks in the scenery, which rose even higher ; these were securely fastened together with sand and cement, and gradually slanted down within eighteen inches of the lake. On top of these rocks ran our natural brooklet, which seemed to rise up in the mountains and flowed down swiftly to the

lake below, with its moss-covered banks, and with rock ferns growing here and there, but before reaching the lake it dropped off in a very pretty splashing waterfall into the water below. This feature alone was a great attraction, as people would stand and study as if wonder-ing where the water came from.

" On the other side of the meadow in the rear was a wind-mill which stood near the lake, and was supposed to pump water from the lake to a tub for the use of the cattle, etc. The lake was about four feet by six feet, and was about six or eight inches deep, and was full of water all the time. Around the edge were laid white cobble stones, with green moss hanging over them, and in this lake swam a school of gold-fish, and a two-mast schooner, heavily laden with ' Frog in your Throat ? ' would toss to and fro by a little ingenious attachment which we had, and this schooner was manned with Frog sailors, dressed in sailor suits and caps, and from the top of the masts streamed banners, ' Frog in your Throat ? 10 cents.' On a heavy rock near the rock-bound coast was a very ingenious light-house, which threw a bright red search-light out upon the water to warn the passing ships of danger, and in the balcony stood a Frog on lookout,

DISPLAY OF MR. R. B. BANCROFT, NEW BRITAIN, CONN.

while on top sat a Frog holding a banner, ' Frog in your Throat ? 10 cents.' A little bridge spans the water from shore to light-house, and the old light-house keeper is seen crossing the bridge, and steps lead from bridge to door of light-house, and from there to the tower. This light-house was our own get-up, and was indeed very unique.

"On the lake were lily pads and Frogs sat on them, or were plunging off at will. We used the Frogs, Japanese lanterns, fans, and adv. strips, etc., you sent us, in every conceivable way we could think of, and the *Human Frog* was a great adv. for us, as he patrolled the streets every afternoon and evening with appropriate signs attached."

The newspapers were very generous to Mr. Bancroft, and most of the prominent ones of his town gave his window write-ups, for which we have no space. On the cover of this book will be found a second picture of Mr. Bancroft's window, taken at night, concerning which he says :

"In regard to the picture we would say that we waited until 11 o'clock at night when the streets were supposed to be deserted to take it, and were then obliged to ask the crowd to stand aside. If we had taken it in

the afternoon we would have shown a swarm of ladies and children."

This bears out our contention that your window can work for you nearly twenty-four hours out of the twenty-four without getting tired.

Individuality in Massachusetts is well represented by Mr. F. R. Pease, of New Bedford. Mr. Pease is a hustler and believes in hammering away regardless of adverse criticism. He says, " Results have warranted me to believe that it pays to exert oneself out of the ordinary, despite the fact that remarks were passed that I was advertising others more than myself."

The order of events here is very plain. While the criticisms were being offered by his competitors Mr. Pease was getting "results." Criticism never yet paid the rent.

A picture of Mr. Pease's " Frog Team " and a few of his interested townsfolk will be seen in the cut. Does it not look as though Mr. Pease's name and individuality are likely to become widely known throughout his section ? Compare his chances with those of his competitor who is striving to secure public attention by his green and pink bottles. The picture of Mr. Pease's

DISPLAY OF J. F. BOMM DRUG CO., EVANSVILLE, IND.

window shows that he, too, has the bottles, but he has used them as a part of his decorative scheme.

His window aptly illustrates the excellent use which may be made of the stuffed frog suits. Concerning it he writes:—

" My window, as you can judge from the photo, is an unusually large one, 20 x 3½ feet, presenting a view from both street and store. The background of the window was made to represent a small grove, the arch above it and life-size Frog being the most conspicuous features. The latter is seen directing the march of the army of frogs from the valley, along the banks of the lake towards the elevated fortress. Upon this lake, the dimensions of which were 6 x 3 feet, may be seen floating toys, boats, fishes, etc. An island is situated in the middle of the lake on which appears a beacon light and a wrecked pilot boat is cast upon the shore."

Mr. Pease also sent a man, dressed in a Frog suit, around on a bicycle. He says:

" This feature was the city's chief talk. At my south end store the crowd so interfered that taking a picture was almost impossible and the 5000 envelope samples soon faded away. People ran out of their houses demanding one, and the small frogs were worn as button hole bouquets for some time.

The cold of a northern winter has not been able to freeze the individual advertising ideas which keep cropping out of the brain and into the window of Mr. J. T. Pepper, of Woodstock, Ontario. He writes " The photograph I am sending you displays considerable thought and ingenuity, and I think that we have produced quite an artistic effect by boring small holes in the floor of the window and inserting artificial plants and flowers. The Frog suit which you so kindly sent me has been stuffed by us with paper, etc., and is made to represent a very large frog. The idea we have tried to depict in the window is a scene from Gulliver's Travels. When Gulliver, on his journeyings, came to the land of Lilliput, being wearied, he lay down and went to sleep. The Lilliputians, finding so large a man in their country, proceeded to tie him down with ropes.

" In our window, we represent the big frog as Gulliver, and the little frogs as the Lilliputians. The little frogs have the big one tied down with ropes. This window has been talked over town, and for days after it was first put in, people, young and old, would stand and gaze and laugh, and the idea that it represented soon spread,

FROG TEAM OF PEASE'S PHARMACY, NEW BEDFORD, MASS.

and people understood what it meant. I am curious to know if any other druggist has thought of this idea. I tell you it is a good one. I intend to leave this window in for two weeks.

"'Frog in your Throat?' has sold better with us this winter than last, and general business is fully 25% in advance."

Daugherty Brothers, of Jeanette, Pa., made one of the most unusual displays that we have ever had presented to our attention ; a display that created no end of talk and improved their business. They write "We believe we have opened a new field of displays ; that of illustrating industries. Our city is entirely composed of glass workers, this being our only industry, and the interest manifested in our display with the Frog glass workers, which accurately picture every operation in glass making, was remarkable. Some few were offended at being represented by Frogs, but they were our best advertisers, as we always had some one to champion our cause, and a crowd was always present to hear the squabble.'' The Jeanette *Dispatch* has this comment to make:

"This year the Frogs have all turned to be full fledged 'cinder heads' and a more complete window glass factory would be hard to find. The base of the window consists of boxes of Frog in your Throat? with the sign 'Chambers & McKee Tank Window Glass Works'

an exact duplicate of the large sign of the Company in front of their works. In the centre of the window is a small window glass tank, at one side of which is a 'blow furnace' and at the other a 'flattening oven,' all correct imitations of the real articles, and built of 'Frog in your Throat?'

"They have a number of 'Frogs' for workmen blowers, gatherers, snappers, flatteners, helpers, carrying boys, cutters, spare blowers, managers, packers, and in fact a full force, and the way they are doing their work is turning some of the old 'cinder heads' green with envy. The factory is equipped with a full outfit of tools, horses, benches, tubs, and in fact everything necessary. The glass cylinders and balls in all stages of development, upon which the Frogs are working so industriously, were all made to order for Mr. Daugherty, and are so correct in detail that one could easily show the whole process of window glass manufacture. At the extreme right of the window is the cutting shop, which is one of the most unique parts of the display. We could give the names of the workmen represented in the department, but guess we had better avoid personalities. One cutter is putting a sheet on the table, another is putting down a light just finished, another looking for 'string,' hookers, packers and carriers are all as busy as if the manager was watching them.

DISPLAY OF DAUGHERTY BROS., JEANETTE, PA.

" A couple of spare blowers are on a bench waiting for jobs and having a friendly discussion to fill in the time. One blower is trying to empty a bucket of their favorite beverage down his throat—oat meal water. A couple of the most natural figures are a snapper carrying a roller from the 'swing hole' to the 'horse' and a carrying boy with a roller under each arm. There are several other unique positions, but we have not room to enumerate them.

"On the whole the window is attracting more attention than any window display ever made in our city."

CHAPTER X

Certainty of Success

Advertising is said to be a lottery, and in the respect that the magnitude of results can never be foretold, it is ; but that it is a lottery in which you may win or you may lose, depends on whether or not you use advertising of the right sort. With some forms of advertising success is certain, and among these a good window display campaign stands conspicuous.

Many druggists pin their faith to newspaper advertising, and some achieve gratifying results, whether the majority get " money back and more " is doubtful.

Results from window displays are surer than those from newspaper advertising for many reasons. Not every newspaper reader is your possible customer, while every passer-by who sees your window is. In your advertisement you describe or attempt to picture the goods that you would sell. In your window you show the goods themselves. You cannot make more than one-quarter of the newspaper buyers read your advertisement. You can make everyone who passes your window, except the blind, take notice of it, and these hearing the comments of the crowd which will be there if your window is good enough, are sure to ask what the matter is, and this is advertising ; but it all depends on the window.

A truly good display is a " puller " that unfailingly gets to work immediately and keeps at it so long as it remains in your window, provided it is not allowed to grow stale.

Our information concerning the certainty of success that comes to druggists who devote time and pains to

DISPLAY OF PEASE'S PHARMACY, NEW BEDFORD, MASS.

making window displays that are striking and attractive is not theoretical, but comes from first hands. In our various prize window display contests we have had thousands of letters from druggists who have competed, and with the exception of two or three cases out of these thousands, everyone reported an increase of business that was marked not only along the special lines advertised in the window, but throughout the entire store.

To make a display that is one of the sights of the town is worth while. Mr. H. R. Baumann, of Washington, Mo., did this and noticed a general improvement in his business all along the line that he says amounted to at least ten per cent. So great was the interest and the pride of his fellow-citizens in this window that he writes, "Any visitors coming to town would without fail be brought to see our window, and parties who had not been in this section of the city for years heard of the display and came to see it." "The window," he says, "cost considerable money, but we did not in the least regret the expense and trouble, as it proved to be a drawing card. The sidewalk would be stopped every evening with the crowds of people trying to see the window, and the rush was so great that many of the people would be forced to go away and come back again some other night. During the day, too, the window was

a great attraction, especially to the country people." This is good work—take notice of it.

Mr. Baumann's window is simple in its idea and elaborate in execution. You will notice the large horse-shoe which is covered with absorbent cotton, on which are nine electric lights with artificial morning-glories used as shades. Within the horseshoe sits the fairy queen, while the Frogs are bowing down to worship. The artificial flowers shown in this display are unusually fine.

Messrs. Caldwell & Bloor, of Mansfield, Ohio, arranged for a very striking window. With a certainty of success that they had a right to expect, they report as follows : "We had largely increased sales during this display, and many comments were made. We spent a great deal of time and thought in preparing it, but feel that it paid." Regarding the mammoth Frog shown in their window they write, "We are sorry we cannot give some accurate scale by which you could better judge the size of the large Frog, which is nine feet high, six feet around the waist, and twenty-eight inches across the top of the head. The framework of this Frog is made entirely of wood, and is covered with a dress suit made of green cloth, except where his under jaw is tinted yellow with anti-kalsomine, and his shirt front made white with the same material."

DISPLAY OF MR. H. R. BAUMANN, WASHINGTON, MO.

In Tarrytown the firm of Russell & Laurie is well known, and has become so to no small extent through their window displays. The following is a description of a display that is well calculated to introduce a druggist to his competitors' customers:

"As a trolley street car road has been the all-engrossing topic of interest in our town, we happily chose that subject for one of our windows, and as our people were divided in the use of Broadway (our most beautiful drive along the Hudson, on which are our handsomest residences) for a route, we appropriately used our Broadway window, and largely advertised 'Broadway Trolley,' 'Franchise Granted,' 'Road Running,' etc. As a matter of fact a franchise was granted during our display, but not to run on Broadway, which made our ads. more effective. After much hunting we found a miniature car containing a motor. The power was applied to a wheel and the rails conducted the electricity,

which was supplied by five cells. It worked automatically, a bar hitting a switch post at each end reversing the motor, sending the car in the opposite direction. The car had a Frog motorman and conductor, and passengers looking out of the windows. The tracks were laid through a tunnel in a mountain of 'Frog in your Throat?' boxes; also at one end of the track was a round house built of the small boxes. The road ran through a park containing a lake filled with gold and silver fish, and around this were arranged Frogs in various attitudes. One was about to leap from a spring board into the water. There were Frogs of all kinds strolling about; lady Frogs with their sunshades; Dr. Frog attending a youngster injured by the fatal trolley, and a pile of skeletons at one end of the track labelled 'Brooklyn,' called attention to another phase of the March of Progress. Our colored porter dressed in the 'Frog in your Throat?' suit, with umbrella, a grip filled

DISPLAY OF MESSRS. CALDWELL & FLOOR, MANSFIELD, O.

with the many souvenirs sent, which he distributed to the children while parading in front of our windows."

Another excellent plan of these enterprising gentlemen was to place a pair of live alligators in a window with a tank for them to disport themselves in, and a profusion of Frogs to keep them from becoming lonesome. They proved a great attraction. These gentlemen write, "We noticed that if we could have something moving it attracted more attention. It was so in this case as well as in that of the trolley."

The certainty of success upon which these gentlemen rely was no false hope. They write, "We did not keep a record of the amount of 'Frog in your Throat?' sold, but we have already sold twice as much as last year, and are confident that it will be three or four times as much."

Mr. George J. Haeussler found that his display produced "a decided improvement, as it brought people into the store who took time to examine the window, and these almost invariably bought something before leaving." Mr. Haeussler's window is seven feet wide and

six feet deep. In the lower right hand corner he arranged a large mirror lake, with Frogs in characteristic attitudes grouped about it—some in the act of plunging in. On the lake appears a swan, and at the edge of the lake a lot of marsh grass, weeds and cat-tails. A brownie appears climbing up one side, while a large Frog chases him. Back of this appears another brownie with a rock raised in both hands above his head, in the act of throwing it at the first brownie. Still further back is a Frog sitting on a log singing the praises of "Frog in your Throat?" Near the centre stands a bittern, a water fowl 18 inches high, with a brownie suspended in his bill by the seat of the breeches. On a toadstool, most naturally made, a Frog appears balancing himself with a spear of grass.

One of the most characteristic features of Mr. Haeussler's window was a brownie "Frog in your Throat?" band composed of six pieces—four horns, a flute and a drum.

The sales from this window display started off immediately with a rush. Mr. Haeussler says they have

DISPLAY OF MESSRS. RUSSELL & LAWRIE, TARRYTOWN, N. Y.

not decreased since. He says that he intends to keep up window displays, as they help general trade.

Harnist & Dale are the Frog Men of Evansville, Ill. They write "Making these displays and changing them frequently has demonstrated to us that although our competitors carry 'Frog in your Throat?' the public in general have considered our store headquarters for that article, and the honor of being considered headquarters for such a prominent preparation as 'Frog in your Throat?' is no slight one." Concerning their display they write: "We have made numerous displays, but this one has proved to be the cracker jack in point of attractiveness, effectiveness and results. The popular phrase 'not in it' is so familiar that every child is enabled to 'catch on' to the point we intend to impress, and the point seems to have been well taken if our sales of 'Frog in your Throat?' is any criterion. It is scarcely necessary to go into descriptive detail, as the display supplies an unlimited number of 'hits,' and the picture speaks for itself. We will, however, briefly mention the Frogs up in a balloon, the astronomer searching the earth for competitors, another weighing the anchor, the dude wearing the plug hat with an open umbrella protecting his complexion, and last the skeleton—one of the 'Frog in your Throat?' rivals suspended from the bottom of the basket, who is strictly 'not in it'."

These gentlemen report a marked improvement in general sales.

In Wheeling, West Virginia, Mr. H. C. Stewart so transformed his lazy windows into active ones that when after a seven weeks' run of the display he took account of stock, the result surprised him. The thorough way in which he impressed his personality on his customers and possible customers as the Frog-Man of his town, not depending on his window alone, but striking out in every direction, is proved by the results to be worthy of imitation. "The people came from all parts of the city," he writes, "and I have entertained both friends and strangers. They came to see the Frog Man's windows." Entertaining strangers is or should be an effort of every druggist, and here is one way to compass it: "I use the signs all over the store where they could be seen," he writes. "Hung thirty-two lanterns from the ceiling, trimmed the shelving with holly, and in fact gave up the entire store to 'Frog in your Throat?' giving every customer a sample of that favorite lozenge. The effort was a trade winner, for during the seven weeks of the display I sold five and three-quarter gross of 'Frog in your Throat?' The figure surprised me, for I had no idea we were selling so much. The windows did the work.

"I had a neat 'dodger' printed, and had a colored man go all over the city in the Frog suit, giving the circulars to every one, and he created an immense amount of talk and excitement; in fact, the crowd following him was so large that he was compelled to go into a store and take the suit off until the crowd dispersed.

DISPLAY OF MESSRS. HARNIST & DALE, EDWARDSVILLE, ILL.

" To explain or describe the windows would he more than I could do, justly, at least; and no photograph would show the beauties of the 'Electric Frog Fountain,' with its Frogs throwing the spray, the flashing electric lights, one color following another and then combining. The railroad train puffing along with its load of Frog passengers, and the combination of colors in the picnic grounds, the gaily-decorated Merry-Go-Round, flowers, lanterns, Frogs, and the steam yacht sailing around the base, all went to make an ever-changing picture that looks bare and hard upon photo."

From Nyack, N. Y., Mr. John D. Blauvelt writes "Again I have made a decided hit with 'Frog in your Throat?' and the result in the way of advertising the goods and in sales has exceeded my expectations. This display has called forth general commendation, and the *Journal*, our leading paper, gave me almost half a column puff on it. This display represents your works at Philadelphia, reproduced in wood, glass and paint, from your cut in back of your book on 'How to Dress Show Windows,' with a train of cars loaded with Frog in your Throat?' coming out of the building. These cars are run by water motor, and the track being circular in form, they are thus constantly in motion, and this cannot help but attract every passer-by.

All about the building are Frog wagons loaded, moss, gravel, etc., etc., and a telegraph line follows the track, and all the surroundings are in harmony with the spirit of the design, and the effect is striking. We are now selling from two to three dozen boxes per day, and the sale is steady."

Mr. Blauvelt reports that after the display was taken from the window he sold for the following three months one gross of "Frog in your Throat?" per week, and that at so late a date as May 11th this article was selling right along.

A pace-maker in the matter of window displays is Mr. A. J. Kaercher, of Allegheny, Pa. He is situated in a location where many electric cars pass the door, and he takes full advantage of this fact in his displays.

We print here descriptions of two of his window displays; both are most excellent.

"DISPLAY NO. 1; FIVE WEEKS
Christmas and New Year

In corner window, on 5 feet revolving stand, a natural bark house 3 by 6 feet octagon shape, trimmed with holly, and illuminated by changeable electric lights. Interior lined with triangular mirrors which multiply everything three to five times to the passing eye.

DISPLAY OF MR. R. M. STERRETT, PITTSBURG, PA.

Third week remodeled and closed with glass doors, handsomely painted in colors. "Frog in your Throat?" etc. on four sides. Eighty-five dozen "Frog in your Throat?" lozenges displayed in window.

The photographs do not begin to represent the display as it appeared to the public. The foliage around the pond was all dark. So much water, plate glass and mirrors made the reflection so great, it was impossible to get a good photograph.

Both my show windows, and in fact the entire store was given over to the display of "Frog in your Throat?" for more than two months. I can report no particularly large sale of the goods on any one day or week, but general results were very satisfactory.

Yours truly,

A. J. KAERCHER."

Notice the large amount of "Frog in your Throat?" displayed; notice also that the results were "very satisfactory." They always are where a consistent and intelligent effort such as this is made.

But although this display had cost time and money in abundance Mr. Kaercher was so well satisfied with the results that he prepared to surpass himself and actually accomplished his purpose.

The description of the display which is given below shows one of the finest mechanical displays ever made. Best of all, the mechanical motion bears directly on the subject of the display. It is "Frog in your Throat?" with emphasis.

Notice in this display that the public desired a continuance of it.

"DISPLAY NO. 2; SIX WEEKS

A natural Frog and Fish pond 5½ feet square; outside covered with green moss, inside lined with a variety of natural water plants; and under foliage, electric lights burning.

On background, arch 6 by 9 feet with twenty-one fine electrical globes, and alternating lights covered with green boxwood plant In centre of arch a large plate glass painted in oil " Frog in your Throat? 10c "; underneath water lily pond.

Over same a fine sheet of water constantly flowing to supply tank for live Frogs and Fish. On back of glass, assorted colored electric lights resembling rain-bow colors after sun shower.

And now last but not least, the Frog himself will be described. **A mechanical device by which he swallows four Frogs every minute, and takes time to chew each one four times, and while doing so blinks his electric eyes eleven times before closing his mouth to receive the next Frog.**

On the whole it looked very natural as the Frog's lower lip dipped in water, and same trickled while in motion.

The public desired a continuance of display, but owing to my rheumatic and bronchial condition had to withdraw it."

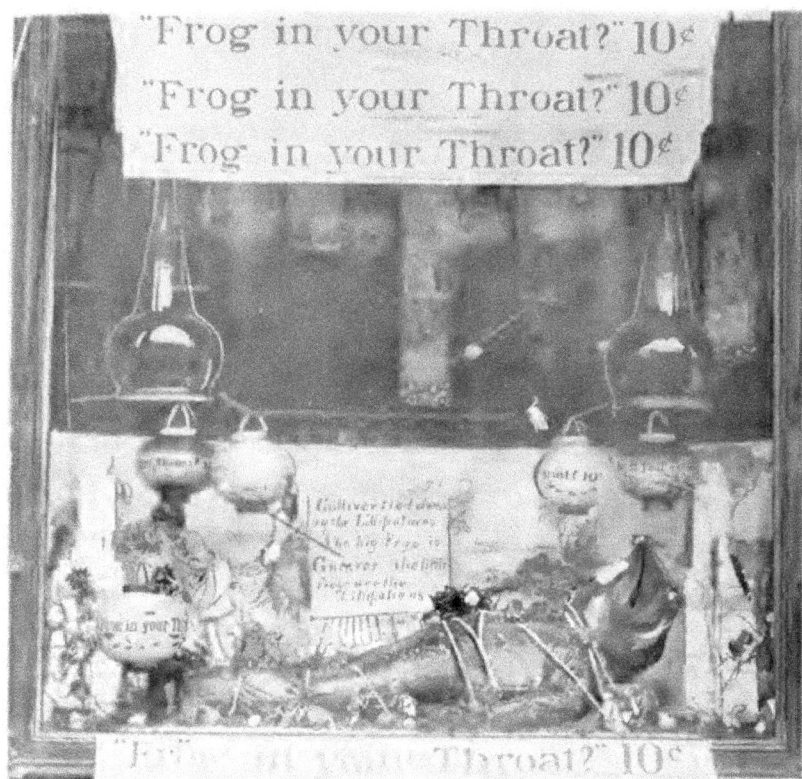

"Frog in your Throat?" 10¢
"Frog in your Throat?" 10¢
"Frog in your Throat?" 10¢

"Frog in your Throat?" 10¢

DISPLAY OF MR. J. T. PEPPER, WOODSTOCK, ONT.

CHAPTER XI

Some Conclusions

In all these talks on window dressing, we have emphasized wherever practicable, the value of the adjunct constituted by the willingness of the average country newspaper editor to generously notice a good window display. The worth of this cannot be overestimated. It is an opinion we have often expressed, that the field for remunerative newspaper advertising to the druggist is exceedingly limited. Our readers know our ideas upon this point, however, and we need not enter into details. Suffice it to say that the class of reading matter advertising embodied in the gratuitous reading notices which (9 out of 10) of the contestants for prizes received from the local paper, is the most valuable advertising in existence, for it invariably brings returns, and costs nothing. Never fail to call your town editor's attention to your displays, if you wish to measure the full possibilities of window advertising.

Another point it is well to remember is the fact that the ideal window display demands everything in accord. Suitable accessories should be provided, and this means appropriate signs, harmony and good taste in the treatment of the subject, and a general all-round filling in of the various parts.

Take for example your window signs. At least one quarter of a window display's worth lies in the quality of the signs or cards which are used to support it. Some druggists say that the more ornamental their signs are the more value they have as advertising mediums. It is a great mistake. Signs should embody the very essence of plainness. They should be so arranged as to be read at a glance. A sign which is fanciful or complicated " wastes its sweetness on the desert air " of unappreciative eyes. In many cases, the signs are the clinching of the attractiveness embodied in the display proper. The latter draws the eye of the passer-by and stays his steps, but the signs go a great way toward determining whether the display is to have the practical result which belongs to

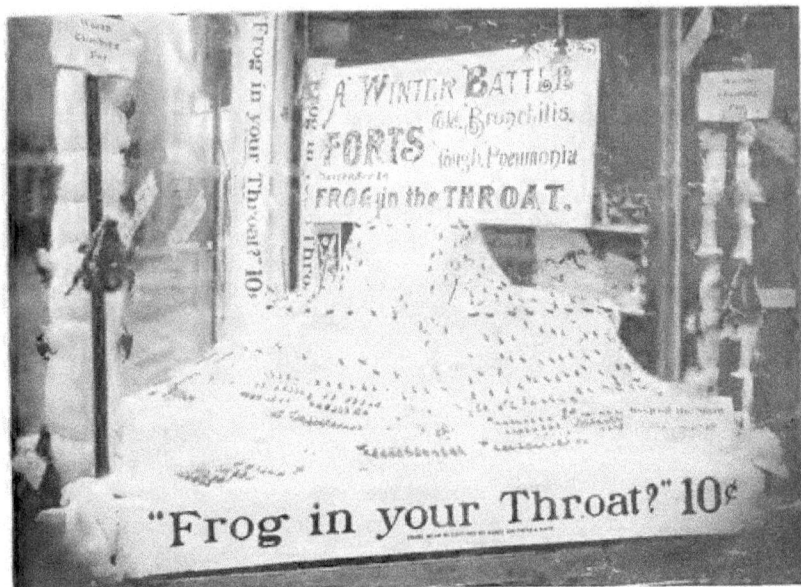

DISPLAY OF MR. W. P. DRAPER, SPRINGFIELD, MASS.

it—the getting of the onlooker into the store to purchase goods. Fancy, ornate signs will never do this in the world. It may do no harm to remind you again that we have a large collection of window signs written by an expert, which we gladly furnish you without charge. Simply select what you wish; and the signs do the rest. In this book you'll see many illustrations showing how good window signs help a display.

There is such a thing as being too ambitious in your displays; remember that. This tendency creeps out in trying to get a twenty-foot display in a six-foot window. Whatever you do, don't jumble or crowd a window display. It's fatal to it, judging by what it could have been if properly treated. Another contrariwise fault is to have the display too small for the window. The thing to do is to have the window and the display fit each other. This is not a science. It merely requires a little care and thought. Don't have several climaxes, so to speak, in your display. Study out one strong effect, and make all the rest of the window lead up to it.

The writer recently saw a display in which artificial birds were used. The birds were like life, while the scenery which formed their background was necessarily but a mere fraction of the proper size. As a result, the birds looked like ostriches. Don't make that mistake. Have your different features in proportion. Have your trees adapted to the size of your houses for instance. Otherwise the picture will be a badly jumbled mixture of

incongruities which will attract ridicule from everybody interested enough to examine it.

It may serve a purpose to say a word on the subject of grouping. The natural tendency is to provide a principal group of some kind, and to place it as near the exact centre of the window as possible. This is wrong. You never saw a great picture yet wherein the chief object was stuck in the middle of the canvass. It is invariably to the right or the left. Use this same idea in arranging a window display, which is after all only a sort of living picture, and must needs follow the general principles of artistic habit.

Too little care is given, as a rule, to this necessity of making everything fit and harmonize. Druggists have been known to use totally dissimilar material in their displays. They would base it on Frogs, perhaps, but would drag in miniature human figures, or brownies, or some other incongruous material that would have been much better omitted. Our idea is to use Frogs and or ly Frogs. The Frogs we use are so constructed that they can be adjusted in all the positions of a human figure. If you want human figures, humanize the Frogs by putting them in whatever position you wish. The effect will be infinitely more amusing, and the material is easier to get and easier to use.

The writer ran across a window display upon one occasion that looked for all the world like a kaleidoscope when viewed from across the street. It was a smeary

"Frog in your Throat?" 10¢

"Going To Beat The Band."

DISPLAY OF MR GEO. J. HAEUSSLER, MANCHESTER, MICH.

flash of gaudy color, and while it attracted by its very hideousness, its attraction was not the sort which brings dollars to the druggist's till. Vivid color is all very well —valuable in fact, but let it be in good taste. Let one tint predominate. If this be green, get it as brilliantly green as you can, but don't introduce a great splotch of red on one side. Other colors are perfectly admissible, but let them be in small patches, introduced here and there harmoniously. After the display is complete, ask your wife or daughter to view it from the outside, from a color standpoint. You can usually use the result as a criterion.

A FEW LITTLE THOUGHTS AT RANDOM.

If there is a theatre in town, see if you cannot borrow there one or two small grass mats. You can make them yourself by staining a coir door mat. Of course, use grass or sod wherever practicable, wherever the display is of a rustic character which demands it. The idea is to be as rational as possible.

Small mirrors can be very effectively used. Borrow or bring from home any old mirrors that you can secure, and place them at the extreme sides near the rear at an angle that will make them face the opposite corner of the front window glass. In this position they will be quite effective.

As to posts in the window. Do not try to leave them out of the picture by ignoring their existence. That will hardly do. Wrap them about with a thin cloth or paper

of the same color as the predominating color in the display.

Some druggists, during their window displays of "Frog in your Throat?" have sent a man through the streets of the town disguised as a Frog.

An important accessory is a mirrored back. This should be secured if convenient, for it makes the whole window look twice as deep, and like the scenery in a theatre, it enhances the entire effect. Every Frog becomes two, every little detail is duplicated far in the rear of the window, and the whole display becomes a picture with a background.

Failing the possession of a mirrored back to your store window, it often becomes a most perplexing question to provide a suitable background for your display. A strip of cloth can be used, either decorated like the scenery of a theatre, or neatly lettered with a border, perhaps, in color. But there is a better plan than having an entire background of cloth. We can supply our customers with a handsome lithographed picture on heavy cardboard which can be very effectively employed as a background of many styles of display. This picture is highly scenic, very decorative and also amusing; can be used alone or in combination with other matter.

Try the effect of making your window-glass into a picture frame. A single five-inch band of paper may be pasted like a border round the outside edges; then leaving a small margin, paste a two and one-half inch band

AN ENGLISH DISPLAY.

inside of it, and (as before) entirely around the four sides of the glass ; inside this paste a one-inch band. Leave from one to two inches of clear glass between the different borders. White paper will probably make the best effect.

Try the plan of spelling out the name of the window display in small boxes or bottles of the article displayed. In the case of " Frog in your Throat ?" it could be easily pelled out in *raised* letters, at least ten inches high. The effect would be truly startling.

Bridges across water are so extremely simple and effective that they should always be used whenever any supposed body of water is introduced. Make the bridge of stiff paper, white card, paste-board, or an old bit of shingle. Use arched or rustic bridges, as they are much more picturesque.

The question of lights at night is worthy of serious thought. Small coiled batteries will supply light for one sixteen-candle lamp, or several miniature lamps of less brilliancy. The power is entirely generated by the coils, and can be maintained for a long period. Lamps and wiring go together. This offers a suggestion for the easy illumination of any features in the display, as a

lighthouse, windmill, bridge, etc. If you haven't electricity handy, a little ingenuity with lamp, candles, Japanese lanterns, or gas-burners, will provide an entirely acceptable effect.

The foregoing remarks apply pertinently to whatever display you see fit to make. And here's another remark you'll do well to keep in mind.

If you want to get the laziness out of your window, don't be lazy yourself. Do this and you will not go at the work in a half-hearted way. Nor will you be downhearted if you don't always find your displays as successful as you think they ought to be. Your failure will only spur you to fresh exertions. You'll study harder to find out in what respects your unsuccessful displays have come short. And, if you get rid of your laziness, you'll not be afraid to change your display frequently. Some druggists leave really good displays in until they become stale.

Don't plead lack of time. There's always lots of time for the man who really wants to do a thing. Materials will gradually accumulate, and as for ideas there's nothing like interest in a subject for sharpening the wits. And don't have lazy people about you.

Chapter XII

Some English Ideas

The whole of the book thus far might bear the title " How 'Frog in your Throat?' Pays the Rent in America", for with the exception of two illustrations, all that has been said and shown has been with reference to the window display talent and enterprise of the American druggist operating on " Frog in your Throat?"

We propose now to show something of what has been done among our English cousins in the way of making their windows pay their rent by means of window displays of " Frog in your Throat?", and, following that, to illustrate and describe some representative displays of other goods by which drugstore windows anywhere can be made to " pay the rent."

The two exceptions to which reference has been made, are to be found on pages 37 and 59 respectively. Each in its way is a representative English display. We inserted them for purposes of comparison. There is nothing " odious " in the comparison one way or other; one hardly needs to be told, however, which are the English displays; the two types are sufficiently distinct. It may be said, perhaps, that the English displays are

1

characterized by what might be termed a good deal of "straight-up-and-down-ness." Everything about them is very precise, substantial, "thoroughly respectable," with a general air of having been set up with much assistance from a foot rule or tape measure.

Illustration No. 1 is not a window display, though English druggists often place it in their windows in conjunction with other matter. They call it a "fix-up", over there, and use it chiefly as a counter advertisement. American druggists might find a hint in this which they could turn to good advantage.

Illustrations 5, 6 and 7, show English ways of using the small Frogs in conjunction with the boxes of " Frog in your Throat?" A little stiff and stilted, perhaps, according to American ideas, but quite effective nevertheless. One beauty about them is the rapidity with

which displays of that sort can be set up. Half an hour's work would be all that would be necessary to make any one of these three displays. Simple little displays like these sometimes accomplish what more ambitious efforts fail to do. Their very simplicity attracts

2

attention. One thing they do is to show very plainly what can be done by the use of the Japanese cotton Frogs alone. These are a host in themselves. You can make them tell any sort of a story. They fit into any kind of a picture. There isn't an attitude within human reach

3

that these Frogs cannot be easily made to assume a close and ludicrous imitation of. And they can as easily be made to caricature human emotions as to imitate human

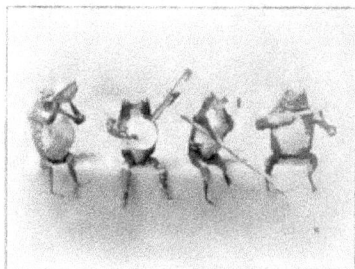

4

5

6

7

8

9

attitudes. Nature was in a jocose mood when she made the first Frog, and there has been something decidedly funny about the "critter" ever since.

Note illustration No. 6 as an example of how well adapted these Frogs are for telling a little story. That particular one is a love story in four acts.

There is first of all the swain in pursuit of his lady love, who is holding up her parasol. Next comes tragedy in the shape of an irate policeman or a jealous rival, probably the latter. In "thirdly" everything is peaceful and serene, while "fourthly" shows an interesting and happy family party.

Illustrations 8 and 9 are two larger displays of the same general kind. Illustrations 2, 3 and 4, are enlarged details of an American display and are good examples of how the Frogs are utilized on this side of "the pond."

Some druggists have the idea that there is no use trying to make a window display unless they have a whole paraphernalia of stuff to work with. It's a great mistake. For elaborate displays no doubt you must have a sufficiency of the right sort of material; but it's a wrong notion altogether that one can't put in a window display with character to it and drawing power also, unless with a big equipment.

A good window display becomes all the more effective an advertisement when it is itself well advertised. Druggists in America have used various methods of letting people know that they had displays in their windows that were worth going to see. One of the most effective of these has been the use of the Frog Suit, and illustration No. 10 shows the manner in which a num-

ber of these suits were also used in England. During the Summer months several minstrel troupes like the one shown in the picture were engaged at various watering places. Their plan of work was to keep the holiday crowds amused with "Frog" songs, "Frog" jokes, "Leap Frog," etc., etc. They would also give away a ticket to every one who "put a penny in the plate," and in this way sent hundreds of people every day into the stores of the druggists, who already had displays of "Frog in your Throat?", for a free sample of the lozenge. This meant splendid advertising for "Frog in your Throat?" and many subsequent sales of that as well as of other goods in the stores of the druggists who had the displays. The troupe shown in the picture advertised one druggist who had bought 20 gross of "Frog in your Throat?" and made a window display, to such good effect that he disposed of the whole 20 gross in a comparatively short time, and sold so many other goods into the bargain that what was an exceptionally bad season for trade generally in his town, proved for him the best he ever had.

This is as good a place as any to make a little digression and emphasize the value of such a novelty as a Frog Suit both for advertising a window display, and for forming part of a window display itself.

A Frog Suit, by the way, for the information of those who do not already know, is a one-piece waterproof garment, which a man or boy can wear over his ordinary clothing. It is made of canvass, painted so as to be in color and general appearance as close an imitation as possible of a Frog's skin. The head piece is separate. It is a big helmet provided with a ventilator,

10

has big bulging eyes, and is a life-like representation on a monster scale of the real thing.

A popular way of using a Frog Suit has been to dress a man or boy in it and send him through a neighborhood carrying an umbrella and bearing on his back some such placard as this "Escaped from Smith's drugstore show window" or "See the fine window display in Jones's drugstore."

On the other hand, either because the law forbade them or because they didn't care to use the suits on the streets, some druggists have preferred to place the Frog Man in their window, mounted on a bicycle perhaps, or trundling a wheel-barrow full of goods, or doing something else to attract attention. The ways are legion in which a Frog Suit can be effectively used in window-display. And it can be used stuffed with excelsior,

newspaper or other material just as well as with a man inside of it.

Look at illustration No. 11 for instance. That shows a stuffed Frog Suit utilized for a display of "Frog in your Throat?" It could be easily adapted to a display of White Pine Cough Syrup, for instance, or other goods of the same class.

Another example of the same sort has already been shown on page 9. That picture illustrates the value of "Frog in your Throat?" to those smokers whose indulgence in the weed gives them the characteristic throat affection known as "smoker's sore throat."

Here is a portion of a letter sent from one druggist to another in which he gives advice founded on his own experience as to how to use a Frog Suit.

"If you are in the business portion of the town, get a small boy, and place him inside the suit to deliver bills, samples of anything you may wish to push, either just outside the door, or have him parade up and down the streets. Place a sign on him "Escaped from Blank's," and get him in the parades of both political parties. Put him in your window on a busy Saturday night and have him cut up all kinds of monkey-shines. If you have a good deal of country trade that comes in by train, have

"Frog in your Throat?" 10 Cents
will stop that Cough.

"Frog in your Throat?" 10 Cents
instantaneous.

"Frog in your Throat?" 10 Cents
will stop that tickling.

"Frog in your Throat?" 10 Cents
Clears your voice in a minute.

11

him meet the trains with a little show card to distribute, neat and with as few words as possible, something the average man will comprehend at a glance."

Resuming the subject of how to support and "back up" one's window display by advertising it throughout one's neighborhood, we must reproduce here a characteristic letter sent to us by an enterprising and original-minded druggist, Mr. H. M. Garlichs, of St. Joseph, Mo.

"I found an elegant way to advertise 'Frog in your Throat?' as follows," he says, "I hired a large two-seated cart and placed in it four negro singers, dressed up in Frog Suits. They played music and sang negro melodies through our principal streets, and I had a man in livery to give away 2000 samples along the route to grown people only. The team was hitched up tandem, and a large Frog was fastened on the back of each horse. Each horse also had a large red wool 'duster' stuck on his head as a plume. The horses and coach were decorated on each side and end with a banner, saying 'Buy "Frog in your Throat?" at H. M. Garlich's drugstore.' I also had a single horse and buggy that I used myself to go ahead and see that the work was well done, and lead the route. I had that team also with banner, and large Frog tied on the horse's back. Every four weeks I also decorate my window with 'Frog in your Throat?' The result is it sells rapidly.

I neglected to mention that each negro singer h one of your Japanese umbrellas over him. I also sa my Japanese lanterns, and every time something n passes my store I string them out in front of the st and they make a nice decoration."

Mr. Garlich's window display by itself would, doubt, have sold goods, but it couldn't have sold many goods had it not been advertised in so energetic

12

way, simply because as many people wouldn't ha seen it.

The illustration on page 48 shows how Mr. Pense.

13

New Bedford, Mass., also appreciated the necessity of advertising his window display in order to bring out its full goods-selling value.

The experienced advertiser never loses a chance of exploiting his wares. And he sees chances where less nimble-witted people see none. All is "grist" that comes to his "mill." A good example of this attitude of mind is afforded by our English agent, Mr. J. E. Garratt, who turned his pet dog into an advertising medium by having him wear about the streets a pretty blanket on which the legend "Frog in your Throat?" was embroidered. And not that only, the dog himself got his name from his master's ruling passion, that of advertising and pushing the sale of "Frog in your Throat?". Illustration 13 shows "Froggie" clad in his advertising blanket.

Illustration No. 12 shows how an American druggist also made use of the dog to help him in his advertising. He had a pair of them and a Frog Suit. He hitched the dogs to a sled (it was Winter time), dressed his boy in the Frog suit and sent him careering through the streets of the town with a placard on his back. It was fun for the boy, and the dogs and the public and the druggist—good fun all around.

14

15

16

Illustrations 17 and 18 show two advertising cars which we had on the streets and in the parade during the Peace Jubilee celebration, held in this city in October, 1898. They are introduced as examples of how effectively the Frog Suits can be employed in parades, etc.

The illustrations do not bring out the details with sufficient distinctness. The car shown in illustration 17 has skilfully postured small Frogs arranged along its top edge. Occupying a pedestal raised above the roof of the car is a monster Frog. Forming a border along the upper edge are a number of " Frog Doctor " automatic figures. The special construction of this car will be noticed ; the roof is raised on supports so as to show the interior, where tablet machines, etc., are on exhibition. Along the top of the body of the car is a row of " Frog Minstrel " cut-outs. Below these and so placed as to leave a ledge, two rows of " Frog in your Throat ?" dummy cartons. On this ledge a number of large cotton Frogs. Below the dummy cartons and concealing the wheels, large " Frog in your Throat ?" muslin signs.

Along the top edges of the car shown in illustration 18 are also arranged small Frogs in various attitudes. Immediately below these are "Frog Minstrel" and " Frog Doctor" automatic figures placed alternately. " Frog in your Throat ?" dummy cartons line the sides of the car, with the exception of a space in the centre which is occupied by a " Red Messina Orange Girl" cut-out, surrounded by a wreath of bunting. Concealing the wheels are " Phénol Sodique " dummy cartons.

CHAPTER XIII

" Strong Man " Window Displays

Deserving to be mentioned in a class of honor by themselves are the rent-paying window displays of various kinds of goods that have been made with what is known as the " Strong Man " for their leading feature.

This Strong Man is a cut-out figure, which is made to simulate in a remarkably natural way certain motions of real life by means of clock-work. We devised the novelty and began its manufacture nearly two years ago. Ever since then it has maintained its popularity as an efficient salesman when used as a window display attraction in conjunction with the goods it advertises.

The figure is beautifully lithographed in several colors, and is so life-like in proportion, color and motion as to be easily mistaken for a living man. A good general idea of it can be gained from illustration 14. The conception typifies health and strength, and the way it is used is in conjunction with window displays of goods that are especially intended for the purpose of making people strong and healthy.

When the automaton has been wound up and set a-going, the arm holding the dumb-bell is steadily raised, the head also moving backwards, so that the eyes of the Strong Man seem to follow the progress of the weight. When the arm has been fully extended, the process is reversed and the arm comes slowly down again. And the figure is constructed so as to hold in the

other hand a lithographed fac-simile of the package of Malt Extract, Beef, Wine and Iron, etc.,—whatever is being displayed as strength-imparting medicine. We have already said, when dealing with the general subject of window displays that there is no surer attraction in a window than some form of animal life. And we instanced the interest that will be taken even in such a dull-looking creature as the turtle when placed in a store window.

Certainly the next best thing to real life is so close an approximation to it as to make people mistake the imitation for the genuine thing. This has happened oftener than once or twice in the case of the Strong Man.

"Everybody admires its life-like movements;"

"It is very life-like and a great many people come into the store to see how it works;"

"Being so life-like makes it a great curiosity."

"People wondered why I had a man in his shirt-sleeves in my window until they found it was an automatic figure;"

Such are some comments taken at random from hundreds of letters which we have received from druggists telling about the Strong Man.

With a striking novelty like this, the difficulty of making a sales-making window display is reduced to a minimum.

Illustration 16, is a case in point. It shows a display which really needs no explanation and only a word or two of comment. There is the Strong Man in the centre. Around him are tastefully arranged whatever goods are to be pushed. On the glass are pasted appropriate signs which are sure to rivet the attention and stick in the memory. Note the Indian clubs and dumb-bells. These are introduced to give emphasis to the story, and bring forcibly home to the beholder the advantage of strength.

The force of contrast can often be effectively illustrated in window display, and there couldn't be a better example than is afforded by illustration 15. What greater contrast could there be than between a lifeless, bloodless, muscleless thing like a skeleton, and the ideas of vigor and vitality which are typified in the Strong Man.

What more natural, therefore, than to place the two side by side, and either by the suggestion alone or by suggestion in conjunction with suitable signs to prove the desirability of keeping as far as possible from the skeleton condition by maintaining health and strength by the use of the goods so effectively advertised.

Illustrations 19 and 20, show two displays which owed their inspiration to the military spirit which was so strongly in evidence during the war with Spain. No. 20 also illustrates the skeleton contrast idea very strikingly and with considerable elaboration.

Here is the way Mr. E. Wunderlich, of New Orleans, used his Strong Man.

"I made a window display with the Strong Man immediately upon receipt of same. It attracted quite a crowd, and, no doubt, helped business. I placed him on a box covered with black cloth, and inscribed the following in white letters: 'Attention! To-morrow evening (Saturday) at 7.30 o'clock sharp this man will begin to lift the 100-lb. dumb-bell. The person guessing the exact number of times the arm goes up will be given a bottle of Beef, Wine and Iron free. It don't cost a cent to guess. All guesses must be in by 7 o'clock'. The

effect was magical. Children going to school noticed the sign and talked about it. When the contest closed at 7 o'clock, there were 560 guesses recorded. When the clock work started the sidewalk was so crowded that it required the aid of a policeman to keep a clear passage. As the work continued, the crowd increased and the excitement was intense. In fact, it attracted more attention than a war bulletin. Does it pay? Well! I should say it does."

We could fill a big book with letters from druggists telling what splendidly successful window displays they made with the help of the Strong Man.

Just a few quotations showing the variety of the goods these displays helped to sell, and the extent to which results proved how true it is that the window can be made to pay the rent.

D. Reed & Son, Pomeroy, Ohio, wrote: "The Strong Man has sold goods for us faster than ever, especially Beef, Wine and Iron, and Compound Syrup of Sarsaparilla. He has made general business unusually good for us this Spring."

Charles E. McPherson, Washington, D. C., had every reason to believe in the rent-paying power of a window in which the Strong Man was working. He says "It has increased the sale of such articles as it can be used with, about 60 per cent."

No wonder Mr. A. C. Walker, Waterbury, Conn., was satisfied. He says "Sold four dozen Extract Malt the first night I had the Strong Man in the window. You may put me down as thoroughly satisfied with my investment."

19

20

CHAPTER XIV

Various Rent-Paying Displays

" Well," some druggist may say, "it is very interesting to see such examples of rent-paying window displays, but I can't buy goods enough at one time to secure such a trade-maker as an automatic Strong Man ; it isn't possible to make an attractive display unless one has something of that sort, or a lot of other good matter."

It is just on this rock of contempt for small things that many druggists allow their ship of opportunity in the way of window display to strike and go down. The idea that it is "of no use " expecting to make a nice window display unless a good deal of money can be spent and a great deal of time devoted to the work, is an utter fallacy. Some fine results have been secured by druggists with but scanty material. Mother wit stood them in good stead and their windows paid so well that before long they were able to secure automatic cut-outs and all the other paraphernalia for elaborate displays. But it is at least open to question if the simplest displays are not the best, no matter how much time and money a man may have to spend in that way.

Illustration 22, for instance, shows a display that is simplicity itself. Anything further removed from expensiveness, or troublesomeness, could not easily be imagined. It is a display of Ten-Cents-Ables. All there is to it is a series of strings suspended from the top of the window and having the goods fastened to them at proper intervals. And there is a pithy sign placed where everybody can see it ; the sign is an important feature of such

displays. The same idea has been used to good purpose for displaying tooth-brushes and other small articles.

A window display may even have a certain crudeness about it without detracting at all from its advertising value. In fact, what might be called the "rough and ready " sort of display will sometimes attract more attention than efforts that are much more pretentious.

The Sarsaparilla display, illustration 24, and the Malt Extract display, illustration 21, are good examples of what is meant. Here again much depends on having snappy signs and arranging them tastefully. When the displays are frequently changed, and this ought always to be the case, it is good policy to vary the more ingenious and elaborate attempts with others of the "homespun" character referred to.

And speaking of varying the character of displays reminds us that there is a certain amount of attractive power in ugliness. But good judgment is essential for making an ugly window display that is also attractive. Take illustration 25, for instance. The display shown there is not a pretty one in any sense of the word, and yet it would attract attention anywhere, especially if interjected among a series of handsome displays.

And now, to illustrate still further how true it is that excellent rent-paying window displays can be made with few, if any, " stage properties," so to speak, except the goods and some clever signs, look at illustration 23. That shows a window display entirely made up of goods we manufacture for the relief and cure of dyspepsia. The goods are attractively arranged ; bright window signs are pasted up ; and, to bring out strongly the " cause "

Malt Extract for Strength

21

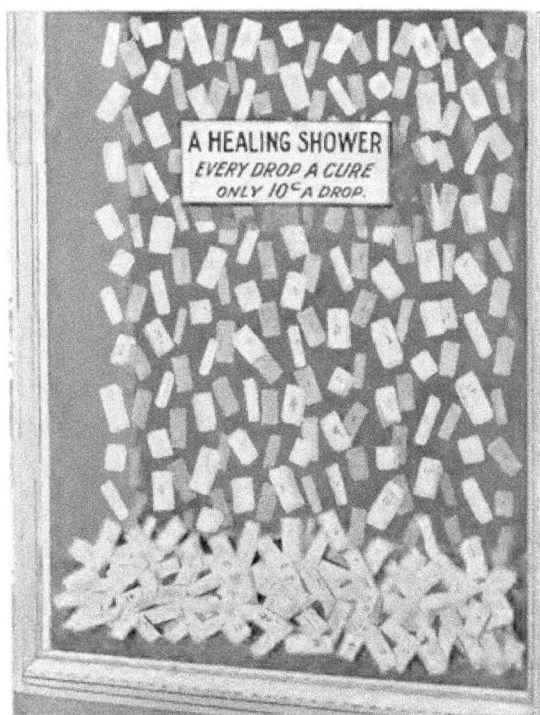

A HEALING SHOWER
EVERY DROP A CURE
ONLY 10 ¢ A DROP.

22

23

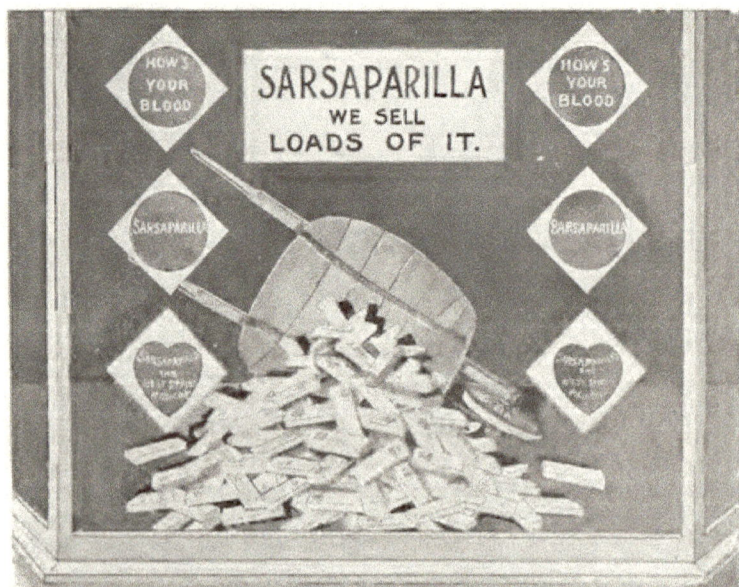

24

and the "effect" in the case, a lobster and two pies are made conspicuous.

Or look at illustration 32, a soda-flavor display. There is nothing there but what every soda-selling druggist has in the store already or can secure at a minute's notice and trifling expense.

Or, take No. 31. That shows a very telling display of Lithia Water Tablets. The point to be made is to emphasize the fact that our Lithia Tablets make the finest possible quality of Lithia Water, and yet are much more economical than the Lithia Water that is offered in bottles. How could it be done better than that display does it? The bottle of Lithia Tablets occupies the fore-

Illustration 34 shows another excellent war time window display in which patriotism and business are harmoniously joined.

The most casual glance shows what an important place window signs hold in display making. Take these away and the effectiveness of the window would diminish by 75 per cent. As we were pioneers in providing druggists with the right sort of window signs, so we have always led the van in furnishing them with the best signs that can be made.

The flags, shields and exploding bomb-shells shown in these war-time window displays are all lithographed signs beautifully done in colors. Illustration 36 shows

EVERY THING IN THIS WINDOW IS POISON

PARIS GR

RYE

25

ground. Around it stand a varied assortment of empty bottles, etc. Contrast No. 1 is that the tiny bottle of tablets holds the wherewithal to make as much Lithia Water as would fill all these large containers. And contrast No. 2, that of expense, is proclaimed on the sign, which tells its own story forcibly enough.

No. 33 shows a display which would necessitate a little larger outlay both of cash and effort. It is a war-time display, and the make-up consists of some photographs of leading actresses, or of other pretty women, a pair or two of cavalry gloves, spurs or other bits of military mementoes, some draped red white and blue bunting for a back-ground, window signs and one of our automatic figures.

a number of suggestions for the effective disposition of such signs. We have many other lithographed signs which we give with goods, and numbers of these are shown in the various illustrations. Illustration 35 shows in outline, how tastefully these signs can be grouped.

The third cover page illustration gives some idea as to both the quantity and quality of the different kinds of lithographed advertising matter with which we supply the druggists who buy our goods to help them make rent-paying window displays. As this is the most profitable advertising for the druggist, we prefer to spend our money that way rather than scatter it in expensive mediums, like newspapers.

The wise advertiser watches times and seasons, and

26

makes his window display fit the particular case. He is talking to the public when he makes a display, and his common sense tells him that it is good policy to talk to people about what they are specially interested in. The pages of this book have described several cases in which a prize-winning window display has "hit off" to good purpose some local event of general interest. The war-time] displays for instance are good examples of another sort. Then, of course, there are the regularly recurrent feast days and holidays of the year. The up-to-date believer in window-display advertising never allows these seasons to slip past unimproved. They are to him hooks of opportunity on which he is prompt to hang his banner of publicity.

Thanksgiving Day, for example. That season is consecrated to good feeling and good fare, and illustration 26 shows a window display that could be made with entire appropriateness at such a time. People will look and smile at the very homeliness of your effort; that is one of the "rough and ready" displays already spoken of, and a good one. Of course, the display could be varied so as to suggest more directly that if too much pumpkin pie, etc., is eaten on Thanksgiving Day you can provide cures for the resulting unpleasantness.

27

OUR FRUIT SYRUPS
ARE
PURE AS EASTER LILIES

28

Illustration 27 shows another ingenious way in which the pumpkin can be used in window display. Pumpkin time, of course, is " Frog in your Throat ?" time also, by reason of the raw cold winds so prevalent then.

Illustration 28 shows how the Easter season can be taken advantage of in making a pretty window display of soda flavors. Easter Monday is a very favorite day with many druggists for opening their fountains. The season typifies newness and fresh beginnings of things. Freshness, purity, simplicity and sweetness are ideas peculiar to Easter-tide. In no better way, therefore, than by some such display as the one shown could the possession of these qualities by your soda flavors be appropriately emphasized. The display is very easily made, and not expensive. And it tells its own story without any interpreter.

An impressive mid-winter window display can be made in the following way; and, of course, it could very easily be specially adapted to the Christmas season.

Have the window wholly inclosed, and cover the ceiling, floor, sides and back of the space with cotton wool. A little dexterity will enable you to arrange this material so as to make it appear flaky. After this has been accomplished satisfactorily, sprinkle it liberally with white frosting to give it the requisite sparkle. Put in a number of red incandescent lamps, and inclose them in globe-shaped wire screens. Cover these screens thinly and loosely with cotton wool, so that, at night, the proper effect may be secured of lights shining out through a veil of fast falling snowflakes.

Hidden at the top and bottom of the window arrange several electric fans, and take care to place them so that the currents of air they generate shall not be impeded. For snow use four or five pounds of goose-feathers The fans will keep them flying.

It will require no great ingenuity to make up the back and sides of the window, so as to represent a street scene. Use some miniature human figures, and have them well sprinkled with snowflakes. Some toy horses drawing sleighloads of Christmas shoppers can be introduced to heighten the realistic appearance of the picture.

By means of such a display you can advertise seasonable goods like "Frog in your Throat?", Syrup White Pine Compound, Cold Cream, Camphor Ice, Witch Hazel and Glycerin Jelly, etc., etc., in a very picturesquely effective manner. And, of course, when you make such displays, don't forget what we have said about window signs. It is the pithy, witty, snappy sign that "points the moral and adorns the tale" of the window display. Put up such signs as these: "After the Sleigh Ride Use Chapped Hands"; "For Chapped Hands and Lips Use Witch Hazel and Glycerin Jelly"; "If Hoarse, take 'Frog in your Throat?'", etc.

And so in like manner with the other days that are marked with a "white stone" in the calendar and stand out from all other days in the year. "May Day," for instance. That is "moving day" in many places. Appropriate displays can easily be gotten up. Call attention to the articles in your stock which are likely to be useful for the various emergencies of such a day. Washington's Birthday, Memorial Day, Fourth of July, and so on,—none of them ought to be allowed to pass without appropriate displays. Not only will this course bring direct trade, it will establish your credit as a wide-awake man of business, who is ever alert to turn all occurrences to good account. To possess a well-earned reputation of this kind is valuable capital. To catch opportunities "on the fly" is the right way to catch them and often the only way. Improve every occasion as it comes and you will be astonished at the result.

Illustration 29 shows a capital window display, which a druggist made while the Klondike fever was at its height. It furnishes another good example of how to accommodate your window displays to the subjects that engross public interest for the time being. The mountains are made of bunched canvass or piles of sand

29

covered with white powder, the effect of which may be heightened by a liberal sprinkling of powdered mica. The log huts are made of pasteboard; the earth around the shaft of the mine may be real earth taken from your garden. And here again is shown the wonderful adaptability of the small Frogs for purposes of window display. They are introduced in this display with wonderfully life-like effectiveness.

Illustration 30 shows a special occasion window display of another kind. It doesn't appeal to sentiment as much as some of the others do, but there's lots of business sense in it. Every druggist knows, only too well, that odds and ends of things will accumulate in spite of him. They are "hang-overs" that are as hard to get rid of as some evening callers. What is to be done with them? They take up room and gather dust. And every day they get worse looking, and, therefore, worth less. This window display shows what to do.

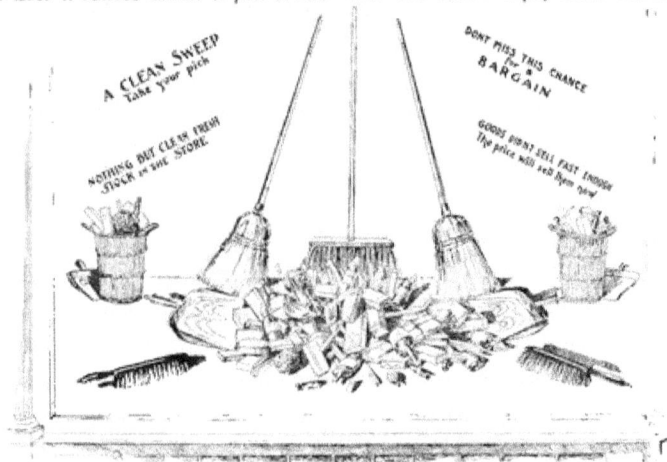

A CLEAN SWEEP
Take your pick

DONT MISS THIS CHANCE
for a BARGAIN

NOTHING BUT CLEAN FRESH
STOCK IN THE STORE

GOODS DONT SELL FAST ENOUGH
The price will sell them now

30

31

32

THE GIRL HE LEFT
BEHIND HIM
DRINKS HIS HEALTH IN
·L·A·W·

33

Three Cheers for the
Red, White and Blue!

34

35

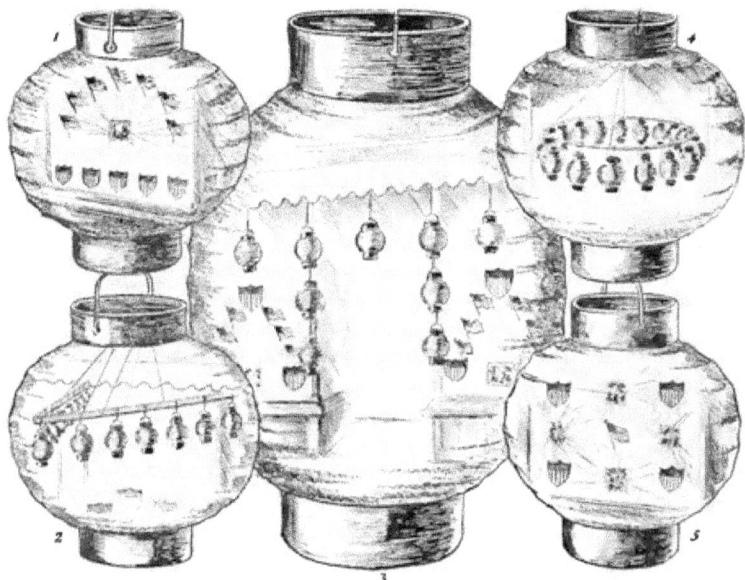

36

INDEX

	PAGE			PAGE
Accessories	56	Frog Suits, stuffed		63
Advertising a Window Display	62	Frog Suits in Parades		64
Agreeable Surprises	37, 39	Frog Acrobats		27, 35
Alligators in Window	52	Frog Aquarium		24
A Magic Phrase	33	Frog Band		52
Animate Nature in Displays	28	Frog Base-ball		34
Arches in Display	30, 47	Frog Battle		40
Artificial Lake	33	Frog Bicycler		45
Artificial Plants	47	Frog Coasting		33
Artificial Snow	74	Frog Firemen		33
		Frog Fishermen		39
Back Grounds	58	Frog Foot-ball		29
Balloon Display	53	Frog Gunners		26
Birds in Window Display	38	Frog Man		53
Boat-house Display	20	Frog Merry-Go-Round		34
Bridges	46, 59	Frog Orchestra		16, 29
Brownies	44, 52, 53	Frog Picnic		22
Burlesque Displays	24	Frog Pond		25, 32
Business Boom	16	Frog Preacher		39
		Frogs in Window Displays	17, 22, 36, etc.
Certainty of Success	49	Frog Snow-ball Fight		33
Cheese Cloth	45	Frog Swallowing Frog		55
Choice of Article for Display	17	Frog Team		46
Christmas Tree Displays	36, 42, 54, 55	Frog Tobogganing		34
Color	58	Frogtown Carnival		21
Colored Bottles Stage of Window Display	4	Glass-making Display		48
Cotton Wool	35, 50	Grouping		57
Creating a "Run"	13	Gulliver Window Display		47
Dogs	64	Hance Brothers & White's Works Display		54
Dyspepsia Window Display	69	Harmony in Window Display		57
Electricity	21, 33, 41, 55, etc.	Horse-shoe Display		50
Electric Fans	74	Hospitable Open Door Idea		5
Electric Frog Fountain	54			
Emphasis	12	Imitation Ice		35
Enthusiasm	40	Impetus to General Trade		17
		Increase of 100 per cent.		20
Ferris Wheel Display	34	Individuality		40
Flowers in Display	45	Ingenuity		35
Foliage in Display	38			
Force of Contrast	68	Keeping Watch on Results		15
Fountain Displays	19, 41			
Frog in your Throat? in England	60	Lake Displays		16, 39, 52
Frog Suits	62	Lanterns		40, 53

Laziness in a Window . . 3, 59
Lazy Windows Made Active . 53
Light-house Display . 45
Lithia Tablets Display 72
Local Events . . . 22

Malt Extract Display . . 69
Mammoth Frog Display 50
Masquerades . . . 42
Mechanical Movement 28
Mexican Frogs . . 42
Mistaken Ideas . 62
Mirrors . . . 54, 58
Mirror-back 58
Mistakes in Display-making . . 57
Moss in Window Display . . 29, 44
Mountains in Window Display . 21, 39

Newspapers 15
Newspaper Notices . 17, 21, 27

Oil-well Display . . 31
Old Castle . . 39
One-idea Method 12
Out-of-Ordinary Exertions . 46
Over-ambitious Displays . . 59

Parades 42, 66
Picture Frame Window . . . 58
Points in Display 35
Poison Window Display . . 69, 72
Police Needed to Clear the Sidewalk . 32
Political Displays . . . 27
Posts in Window . . 58
Post-Mortem Decisions 12
Potent Questions . . 10
Pretty Displays 28
Proportion . . 57
Public Fountain 43

Reading Notices 56
Results of One-Idea Method 15
Rough-and-Ready Displays . . 69

Running Water in Display 28
Rustic Display . . 14

Sarsaparilla Display . 69, 71
Sawdust 26
Science of Window Dressing 4
Seven-weeks Display . . 53
Ship-canal Display . . 25
Show Window Evolution 3
Signs . . . 69
Simple Displays . . 60
Skeleton Displays . 37, 68
Special-Day Displays . . 75
Spelling Out a Name . 59
Street Display . 64
Strong Man, the . . 66
Strong Man Displays . . . 66, etc.
Stuffed Frog Suits in Display . 47

Telling a Story by Window Display 60
Ten-Cents-Ables Display . . 69
Toy-store Ideas . . . 35
Trolley-car Display . . 51
Tunnels 30, 51
Two Sorts of Advertising . 40

Ugliness in Displays . 69
Unsecured Results 38
Use of Real Sod 30

Value of Curiosity 41
Value of "Talk" 41
Visitors Brought to See Displays 30

War-Time Displays 68, 69, etc.
What a Window Is 9
What to Do with "Hang-Overs" . 75
Wind-mill Display 45
Window Display a Business Tonic . 12
Window Displays and Dignity . . . 10
Window Display vs. Newspaper Advertising 49
Windows as Light Admitters 3
Windows vs. Doors . 5

www.ingramcontent.com/pod-product-compliance
Lightning Source LLC
Chambersburg PA
CBHW021427090426
42742CB00009B/1284